THE TIME OF THE CANTON

A Sea Story

Michael McLoughlin

Dedicated to the greatest man I've ever known, my father, James McLoughlin

Cover Photo by
Angela Kelly - wildatlanticimagesaok

CONTENTS

PROLOGUE

I t was the summer of 1940, and the war was not yet a year old. Hitler had begun the epic conflict in September of the previous year with his invasion of Poland. It followed many deals with the dictator of Germany and many broken promises that he wanted only so much of this or that and nothing more. Then on September 1st 1939 he invaded Poland after staging a false flag attack on his own border guards by Nazi SS troops disguised in Polish uniforms.

Finally England and France felt that he had gone too far and Poland was the last straw. The fact that Russian troops under Stalin, who was Hitler's ally at the time, invaded Poland from the east just weeks later on September 17th is somewhat lost in the history of it all. But England and France felt that to declare war on Russia was a bit more than they could handle. Diplomacy can get technical, and they had promised Poland help against Hitler's aggression specifically. They failed to come to the aid of Poland and the country was crushed from two sides.

Russia was claiming its part of Poland as it had done with Prussia and Austria a century before. Stalin was waiting for the Wiermacht to defeat most of the Polish military which it did in 6 weeks. The Soviet Army was smarting from a humiliating defeat that the Poles had inflicted on them in the short but forgotten bloody struggle known as the Polish Soviet War. The Spanish Civil War and Mussolini's invasion of Ethiopia as well as the Japanese invasion of Manchuria and China got most of the pre-war press, but there were other conflicts that whetted the weapons and armies of nations as they prepared for war just as had happened a mere 25 years before. Hitler and Stalin divided Poland.

On 22 June 1941 when Hitler turned on his former partner in Poland's invasion and attacked the Soviet Union, Stalin was quickly taken into the Allied camp and "Uncle Joe" took on a new role since "the Enemy of my enemy is my friend". Before Hitler's invasion of the U.S.S.R. the Communists in America were all for pacifism and neutrality since Hitler and Stalin were allies. After the invasion, (Operation Barberossa), they were screaming for the U.S. to get involved. Six months later the attack by the Japanese on Pearl Harbor made it a moot point.

This goes to show how politics and diplomacy can make strange and strategic bedfellows and unfortunately the vast majority of the people who will be most affected by these deals have no clue as to how or why their lives are being uprooted and bargained away. It's all pretty ironic that the war in Europe started because of the Allies commitment to Poland's independence, and after the war was over, when the smoke cleared and the rubble was pushed away Poland remained under the rule of one of their original invaders for fifty years.

The treachery of the Allies toward Poland at the end of the war is inexcusable. The British were so concerned with upsetting Stalin, who had taken over Poland, that they didn't invite the Free Polish armed forces to the victory parade in London. The Poles had fought valiantly as a nation in exile with over two hundred thousand troops on land and sea and in the air. They fielded the fourth largest Allied army in Europe after the Soviet Union, the United States and Great Britain. Their contribution even before the war was immeasurable since in 1932 and up to the invasion, Marian

Rejewski, Henryk Zygalski and Jerzy Różycki at the Polish General Staff's Cipher Bureau in Warsaw had developed techniques and devices that went a long way toward cracking Germany's secret code.

The Poles distinguished themselves in the air in the Battle of Britain. The Polish 303 Fighter Squadron claimed the highest number of kills than any other Allied Squadron. The Army fought in many major battles including the D-Day invasion, the battle of Monte Casino as well as the ill planned Operation Market Garden and many others. The Polish Navy, as well as taking part in the demise of the Bismarck, sank 12 enemy war ships, including 5 submarines, damaged 24 more, including 8 submarines, and shot down 20 aircraft as well as sinking 41 merchant vessels. Considering the work of the code masters it would be safe to say that without the Poles in Exile the war may have had a very different outcome or have lasted longer.

Stalin was a cruel dictator every bit the equals of Hitler when it came to a disregard for human life. He once told the U.S. Ambassador, Averill Harriman that, ""The death of one man is a tragedy, the death of millions is a statistic." Being responsible for the death of over forty three million people he was an expert on the subject. Yet the Allies needed him to keep the Germans battling a war on two fronts. There is many a man that "sleeps in the deep" after losing their lives on American and British ships bringing vital supplies to the Soviet Union.

It's doubtful if the Russians could have withstood the German onslaught without Allied ships that sailed the icy waters and braved the attacks by planes, ships and U-boats running the gauntlet on their way to Archangel and Murmansk. The U.S. gave over 11 billion dollars in aid to the Russians. This was quite a fortune considering the value in comparison to modern money since $100 in 1946 was equivalent in purchasing power to over $1,200 in 2017.

American made planes were flown to Alaska by men and women

pilots and then were picked up and flown to Siberia and on to the Eastern Front by Russian and American pilots stationed there. Supply lines of tanks, trucks and food were established through Iran. Two English words were known to every Russian; "Studebaker", (an American truck), and "Spam".

Allied help and Hitler's hubris was what saved the Soviet Union. When viewed through the eye of history, if not for the awful tragedy of it all it would be laughable when you think of just exactly what war is. One generation's enemy becomes the next generation's ally after nearly annihilating each other and former allies become deadly enemies.

Hitler's blitzkrieg overran just about all of Western Europe and England stood alone against the Furor and his lust for power. The situation looked very bleak with the fall of France. With his ally Mussolini as Fascist dictator of Italy claiming territory in Africa, Franco another fascist, as a "neutral" ally controlling Spain, and Japan as one of the Axis powers conquering vital parts of Asia, Hitler seemed unstoppable.

By controlling France the Germans had a window directly to the Atlantic from ports like Brest, Bordeaux, Saint Nazaire, Lorient and others. Their U-boats could intercept ships bound for Britain without having to sail past England and its protective navy which was far superior to the German's above the waves. The U-boats were taking a heavy toll. When it was over, Churchill said that the only thing that really frightened him during the war was the U-boats.

On the 3rd of September 1939, 2 days after the invasion of Poland, England and France declared war on Germany. The day war was declared the German U-boat U-30 under the command of Captain Fritz Julius Lemp was on patrol west of Ireland in the North Atlantic.

Lemp came upon a ship that night running with her lights out and on a zigzag course and he immediately took her to be an armed merchant, which was fair game within the rules of war. He called all men to battle stations. He followed her and at 19:40, between Rockall and Tory Island off the northwestern coast of Donegal, he fired two torpedoes at the ship.

The first ripped her amidships, the second became stuck half way in the tube. U-30 had been fitted out with new magnetic detonators and the crew knew that when the propeller on the torpedo stopped they would have succeeded in sinking the first enemy ship of the war as well as being the first German casualty of the war by blowing themselves to bits with their own torpedo. The situation was grave and Lemp wisely ordered all stop, and the crew managed to push the torpedo out of the tube.

It was only after the stricken ship began sending out her distress signals that Lemp realized he had made a terrible blunder. He had attacked a British passenger ship, the Athenia bound from Glasgow to Montreal. She was carrying 1100 civilian passengers on holiday including over 300 Americans as well as the crew. She went to the bottom with 112 killed in the attack, 28 of which were Americans.

Then over the radio Lemp received the order to maintain all rules of engagement on the high seas regarding passenger ships and unarmed freighters. This entailed stopping the ship, sending out a boarding party that would inspect the cargo and ships papers for "contraband", and if found the crew was given the opportunity to abandon ship in their lifeboats and the ship would be sunk by torpedo or gunfire.

He left the scene without picking up any of the survivors and later swore four of the crew to secrecy when he had to put them ashore in Iceland due to wounds received in a battle with British destroyers and aircraft on their second cruise. The Germans feared that the incident might bring the U.S. into the war on the British side as the Lusitania sinking had turned American sympathies against Germany in the First World War.

When Lemp returned to Germany he found himself in some hot water, and was summoned to make account for his actions. He had not contacted Germany for fear of disclosing his position. The Germans thought they had no U-boats in that area because they had not received any messages and were disavowing the sinking and blaming it on Churchill as an attempt to sway neutral countries against Germany. But Roosevelt had pledged the U.S. to neutrality despite the Athenia affair and Lemp found himself again at sea as commander of U-30.

The affair was covered up, the entry was taken out of the ships log, and the Nazis announced that it was the English that had sunk the Athenia. The British felt that Germany had returned to unrestricted submarine warfare as they had in the last war. The truth finally came out at the Nuremberg Trials in 1946 when Admiral Donitz admitted to the sinking by U-30, and the subsequent cover up in a statement he read at the trial of Grand Admiral Reader.

So Lemp had fired the first shot of the war against England and began what came to be known as the Battle of the Atlantic which raged on throughout most of the war with the U-boats enjoying an early advantage until the convoy system was perfected.

Before Pearl Harbor, America's "Lend Lease" program helped England acquire some old destroyers to try to keep their vital lifeline with Canada and the United States open. The Brits also assigned some old warships to convoy duty, but after Japan's attack on Pearl Harbor when the U.S. officially entered the war the "Happy Times" for the U-boats was over. A full three-quarter of those who sailed out on those once feared craft never returned thus racking up the highest losses of any units on either side in the war.

THE STAGE

T hroughout history during and after some great cataclysmic event the people have felt that it was the end of the world. From wars and fallen empires; pestilence, earthquakes, volcanic eruptions, and famine: down through the ages people experiencing these disasters thought it was the Apocalypse.

For the people of Europe after the Great War which lasted from 28 July 1914 to 11 November 1918, it was no different and the situation fulfilled all the prophecies. Never before in the history of the world had there been death and destruction on such a scale as had taken place. The total number of casualties was over 41 million. Eighteen million were dead and 23 million wounded. About 9 to 11 million military and between 5 to 6 million civilians lost their lives. Towns, cities and farms were destroyed and the inhabitance found themselves plodding along roads with whatever belongings they had searching for what was once their home or for someplace else to live.

The war brought famine. Blockades and economic upheaval caused the starvation of countless victims, especially in Russia. To add to all this misery influenza, known historically as the "Spanish Flu", started in 1918 toward the end of the war and spread throughout the whole world infecting over 500 million people even in places as far removed as the Pacific Islands and the

Arctic. Between 3 to 5% of the World's population perished.

There was much unrest in many parts of Europe. Riots and street battles were taking place between communists and conservative groups. The new nation of the Union of Soviet Socialist Republics which was formerly the Russian Empire had made a separate treaty with Germany and the "Central Powers" in March of 1918. This took Russia out of the war as planned by Lenin and the German agents who gave him money and safe passage to start his Bolshevik revolution. After the war the U.S.S.R. began sending agents all over the world to stir up social and economic unrest which is part of their modus operandi to spread communism.

There was a bloody civil war in Russia between the Communist Bolsheviks, known as the Red Army, and those loyal to the Czar, known as the White Army. The communists decided to go the way of the French during their Revolution in 1789, and eliminate the source of any loyalty to the crown by murdering the whole Romanov family in a dingy basement.

The Czar, Czarina, their four daughters and the young Alexi who was heir to the throne were killed by brutal drunken Red Army soldiers who botched their evil intent and had to go back to shoot and bludgeon them to death before being dragged off and buried in an unmarked grave. They went on to hunt down and kill as many of the Romanov's and extended family as they could find in their effort to wipe out any connection with the past.

Several European nations as well as the United States, Japan and China sent troops to aid the White Army. This fact helped to give rise to the "them or us" kind of mentality of the communist leaders throughout their hold on Russia and their satellite states until the demise of the Soviet Union at the end of the last century.

The fact that the tenets of communism call for world domination made for much trouble in Europe as competing sides struggled for power. Some of these countries had never known democracy and they wanted it. The communists preached democracy but knew that their socialist scheme would never be accepted by a free people with a right to vote. They focused instead on the evils of capitalism and the benefits of Socialist Communism, where the State owned everything and everyone was in one big labor union with no private property.

"From each according to his ability, to each according to his needs" was the mantra popularized by Karl Marx in his Communist Manifesto. Communism seems like a wonderful idea where everyone is equal; no rich, no poor, with everyone living in Utopian bliss. But a large community is going to need some organization and rules to go by. That means someone has to be chosen to oversee and direct the community.

This immediately establishes another class of people who are above the masses. Let's call them "Commissars". As the community grows, the Commissars will need someone to "guide" them. Before you know it, everyone isn't as equal as they were supposed to be. Just like the fruit in the garden, communism looks so good and promises everlasting pleasure, but to take one bite is enough to realize that you have partaken in something that was created in the fires of Hell.

Two important words are left out of their seemingly high sounding proposal. "Take" and "Give". They will take from those who can produce and give to those who can't. Charity is a blessed thing, but "Charity" translates into "Love" and forced love is no love at all and only causes resentment. Charitable organizations and religious communities have been providing for those less fortunate for years. Free enterprise and Capitalism have lifted more people out of poverty than any other economic system in history.

Under communism private property and free enterpise must be abolished and of course the government decides what kind of work is most suited for you to do and just about everything else in life all for the good of the state. There is no incentive to better yourself. People become just a cog in the wheel that drives "The State". Ants live like this!

Russia started "Collectives" where the peasants were forced to give up any private land and live on farms where everything is doled out to them and the rest taken to distribute. Needless to say this met with much opposition especially in Ukraine, and the result was mass murder through what is known as the "Holodomor" or "The Terror Famine". An estimated 10 to 12 million Ukrainian people were purposely starved to death by Stalin. Anyone who disagreed with these programs would sometimes just "disappear". It was death or exile to Siberia for those who would not tow the party line.

The Soviet Union sent out it's operatives far and wide. They infiltrated the most important institutions in western culture such as education, science, business, unions and even the Catholic Church. The general belief is that the West won "The Cold War". I disagree although we did succeed in bankrupting the Soviet Union. With the rise of the Solidarity movement in Poland under Lech Walesa, and the combination of Reagan, Gorbachev and Pope John Paul II the Soviet Union did collapse, but the seeds that have been sown by this "Evil Empire" still disrupt our world and will continue to do so for a long time.

The most important institution that they infiltrated is education. In America during the 1930's they just about took over the AFT, (The American Federation of Teachers). Under pressure from the AFL, (American Federation of Labor) they were forced to eject 3 unions including AFT Local 5 the New York City Teachers Union for being dominated by communists. They still have a hold on teacher's unions. Left wing anti-war protesters from the "60's and "70's many of whom were communists or sympathizers, are now teachers and professors.

As an example, prominent "Domestic Terrorist", Bill Ayers , a former leader of the "Weather Underground", (a self avowed

Communist organization dedicated to the overthrow of "Imperialism"), is now an "elementary education theorist". Ayers and his wife Bernadene Dohrn were wanted for years by the FBI for bombing the New York City Police headquarters, The Capital Building and The Pentagon. They were aquitted since the FBI used wiretaps and property searches without warrants. All weapons and bombing charges against the Weather Underground were dropped including those against Ayers. How many more of these people are "educating" our children?

They indoctrinate the youth with propaganda that makes socialist-communism appealing in spite of the historic evidence that far from the promised Utopia, it only brings poverty and misery. They paint a pretty picture where everything is free and everyone is taken care of by "The State". They never mention the poverty, lack of freedom and oppression in communist countries throughout the world. They never teach that free enterprise leads to competition which breeds ingenuity leading to better, safer products.

It's hardly known to anyone that in 2018 we reached a milestone in human history. For the first time the world's population has reached a point where the majority is no longer poor. Due to capitalism and free enterprise the world is now trending toward middle class. People working in rice paddy's have cell phones with them. Tribes that use blow-guns in Amazonia can keep track with smart phones of poachers and illegal logging on their land using GPS. Absent some cataclysmic disaster, whether people want to admit or not, the world is getting better.

During the 1920's, in Italy a movement called Fascism came to power under Benito Mussolini. The people grew tired of the constant upheavals and lack of common services and the communists were making great strides to take over the government. Fascism takes its name from the "Fasces" which were carried before the legions on parade during the Roman Empire. It is an axe with a bundle of sticks tied around it and was the symbol of authority.

Fascism is dictatorial with one leader making the decisions. This is the usual end result of constant turmoil and violence when people are willing to give up some rights in order to have peace. Many found that giving up "some rights" eventually leads to the loss of all.

Mussolini was a newspaper man before the Great War. He enlisted and served in an elite unit where he was decorated and then finally discharged due to wounds he received. He was originally a socialist but came to believe that class warfare was not the answer to the problems Italy faced. Instead he preached a patriotic nationalism that would echo the great days of the Roman Empire. Of course he would take the part of Emperor and dubbed himself "Il Duce" or "The Leader".

He and his followers marched on Rome in 1922 with an armed insurrection in mind. The Prime Minister wanted to declare a state of siege, but instead the king appointed Mussolini as Prime Minister thus handing over power to the Fascists.

He ruled constitutionally until 1925 and then showing his true colors he openly became a dictator. Opposition parties were abolished and freedom of the press disappeared. Within five years Mussolini had by legal and illegal means taken complete control of the government and began building up the military.

He instituted government work programs that were not always economically sound, but did get people to work. He did much to suppress the Mafia and made government services more reliable. His suppression of communism found favor with the Catholics which made up the great majority of the country. He invaded and conquered Ethiopia whose military was no match for a modern mechanized army. The League of Nations which was set up after the war as a way to settle international disputes was toothless and did nothing to aid the ancient African land.

In Germany, after the Kaiser was forced to abdicate and the Weimar Republic was established the economy was in ruins. Inflation set in and people were literally taking wheelbarrows full of money to the store to buy a loaf of bread. The money wasn't worth the paper it was printed on and some used it to start their fires. In 1914, 4.2 German marks was worth about one American dollar. Nine years later, it was 4.2 trillion to one. People were taking suitcases and bags to work to collect their wages. One story had it that a man had his suitcase full of money stolen and found all the cash dumped out on the street.

After a reshuffling of the debt and creation of a new currency in 1924 Germany reached a point called the "Golden Twenties" that was comparable to the "Roaring Twenties" in America. In France, it was known as Les Années folles. This was "Party" time! Old norms were pushed aside and fashion, music, art and attitudes reflected loose living. Just about everyone was investing in the Stock Market and with Wall Street creating millionaires it was an incentive to invest even more. But powerful political forces were at work behind the scenes and most people were unaware.

Adolph Hitler was living in Munich when the war began. He enlisted in the German army and through an administrative error he was accepted although he should have been returned to Austria, his homeland, to serve in their army. He was made a dispatch runner and participated in many battles. He was awarded the Iron Cross 2nd class and later given the Iron Cross 1st class which was rarely given to a soldier of his rank. He was recommended for it by his Lieutenant who was a Jew named Hugo Guttmann.

He was praised by his commanding officers. He also was wounded in the thigh by a shell that hit the dispatcher's dugout during the Battle of the Somme and received the Black Wound Badge. He was recovering in a hospital after being blinded in a mustard gas attack when he heard the news of Germany's defeat. He was crushed and later said he relapsed into blindness after hearing the news.

With the humiliating Treaty of Versailles which just about laid the blame for the whole war at Germany's feet and the tremendous monetary reparations levied on them as well as the loss of territory and dismantling of the armed forces; this disgruntled Corporal vowed that he would avenge his adopted country.

Many of the people and especially the veterans of the war felt that Germany had been stabbed in the back by politicians, bankers, communists and Jews. Since Karl Marx was ethnically a Jew it was easy to associate communism with the Jews. Unfortunately most Anti-Semites don't associate Christianity with the Jews.

Before the war he wanted to be an artist but was turned down twice by the art Academy in Vienna. His drawings were good, but he had trouble depicting people and he was told he should try architecture instead. He sold postcards and drawings of the city as well as working as a day laborer just to survive. He lived in flop houses and struggled to make a living. He moved to Munich, Germany after receiving the final part of his father's estate and joined the German army at the outbreak of the war.

Now that the war was over, and finding himself without any higher education or skill, he decided to stay in the army and he became an intelligence agent. He was ordered to infiltrate the German Workers Party, (DAP). At a meeting of the party the chairman was impressed with Hitler's oratory and gave him a copy of his pamphlet, "My Political Awakening". It contained anti-Marxist, anti-Capitalist and anti-Semetic ideas

Hitler's commanding officers ordered him to join the party. At this time he became more anti-Semitic and believed that Germany's problems could be solved by getting rid of all the Jews. About this time the DAP changed its name to the Nationalsozialistische Deutsche Arbeiterpartei (National Socialist German Workers Party; NSDAP). Hitler himself designed the party banner consisting of a black swastika in a white circlular background on a red field.

He designed uniforms for party members which gave a flare to their meetings and parades and the street fights and riots that they were often in. He became more involved in the party and left the army in 1920 to work full time for the NSDAP or as it came to be known, the Nazi party. He went on to become the chairman. Dietrich Eckart, one of the founders of the party and a member of the Thule Society became his mentor and he was introduced to many influential people in Munich.

At the end of the 19th and the beginning of the 20th century many people were influenced by new scientific discoveries which gave them an excuse to abandon traditional religion. But since humans are made of spirit as well as body, many still felt a need for some contact with the spiritual world and turned to seances, tarot readings and just about anything to do with the occult.

Belief in New Age religions spurred on by Theosophy and mixtures of mystic Hinduism and Buddhism were very popular especially among the upper classes. The Thule Society was an example of this with its reversion to ancient Germanic paganism and its myths and rituals. It emphasized racial purity and the Germanic people as the "Master Race". Many Nazis were members of the Thule Society and it was instrumental in the success of the Nazis rise to power.

Hitler rejected Christianity, regarding it as a sect of Judaism and longed for a return to the old Germanic Pagan religion, hence his love for Wagner's operas. Almost as if with diabolic intent he eventually orchestrated his Third Reich as if to imitate Wagner's „Gotterdammerung" or "Death of the gods" where Valhalla bursts into flames consuming the gods and cleansing the Earth, making it ready for a new start.

His natural gift for oration as well as coaching from actors made him a popular speaker in the beer halls and party meetings at first centered in Munich. His main message was one of strong nationalism, with the usual emphasis on how the nation was "stabbed in the back" by the politicians, financiers and especially the Jews. Criticism of the Versielles Treaty, Capitalism and Marxism were part of the message. Boosting the pride of the Germans as the true Arian race superior to all others was an integral part of the meetings.

When he felt strong enough he organized a coup d'état. With the help of World War I General Erich Ludendorff they started what became known as the "Beer Hall Putch". The Nazis wanted to emulate the Fascist's "March on Rome" in 1922 which brought Mussolini to power. They planned to take over the government in Bavaria and then Berlin. They occupied the local Reichswehr and police headquarters but neither the state police nor the army came to their support. During the ensuing battle with the army who were called in to suppress the uprising, several of the Nazis were killed.

The coup failed and Hitler was sentenced to five years in Landsberg Prison for High Treason. He was well treated by the guards, allowed visitors and was given special privileges. He was pardoned by the Bavarian Supreme Court against the prosecutors wishes and ended out serving about one year for his crime. The Bavarian government wanted him deported back to Austria but the Austrian government refused stating that his former service in the German army voided his citizenship. Hitler formally renounced his Austrian citizenship on April 7th 1929.

After his release from prison he found himself to be even more popular, but the Nazi Party was banned for a while and economic times were better which took away one of their main issues. The Stock marked crash of 1929 put the economy back on the list of grievances of the German people. What resulted was a financial depression that affected the whole world. People who were millionaires one day were paupers the next. Shantytowns grew up all over the United States and people were lining up for soup kitchens and selling apples on the street corners. Banks and businesses all over the world failed.

In Europe the situation was even worse than in America. Pitched battles were fought in the streets by opposing factions. In order to lift the ban imposed on the party and himself personally, Hitler promised that he and the Nazi party would abide by the democratic process. Eventually the Nazi's gained more seats in the Riekstag, the German Parliament, and although they weren't the majority party they were needed to form a government.

Germany's venerable president, Paul von Hindenburg, at the urging of many industrialists and businessmen appointed Hitler Chanceler of Germany. They wanted Hindenburg to appoint a leader of a government "independent from parliamentary parties", that could turn into a movement that would "enrapture millions of people".

Not long afterward the Riekstag building mysteriously burned down and it was blamed on the Communists. This gave Hitler an excuse to urge Hindenburg to enact emergency laws for the good of the country. Germany's previous governments had at times issued emegency orders curtailing certain rights. Hindenburg issued the Reichstag Fire Decree. It suspended basic rights and allowed detention without trial. The German Communist Party (KPD) was suppressed, and over 4,000 members were arrested. This brought about a crack down on any opposition.

Hindenburg died on August 2nd 1934. Just one day before his death the cabinet had enacted the "Law Concerning the Highest State Office of the Reich". This law stated that when Hindenburg died, the office of president would be abolished and its powers merged with those of the chancellor. Hitler thus became head of state as well as head of government, and was formally named as *Führer und Reichskanzler* (Leader and Chancellor). He became commander-in-chief of the armed forces. After Hindenberg's death, the traditional loyalty oath of soldiers was altered to affirm loyalty to Hitler personally, by name, rather than to the office of commander-in-chief.

While in prison he dictated his book, "Mein Kampf", "My Struggle" to his deputy, Rudolf Hess. It was dedicated to Thule Society and party member Dietrich Eckart who had been his sponsor. It was part autobiography and also his plan for Germany as a pure Arian race. Hitler as well as many other people in those days believed in Eugenics. This pseudoscience was taken very seriously by the Western World in the later part of the nineteenth century and the beginning of the twentieth. It was taught in schools including the top Universities. Exhibits and tests at fairs informed people if they were of the "right stock". This had much more to do with racism and population control than science.

Based on a book written in the 18th century by Thomas Malthis, "An Essay on the Principle of Population", his followers known as "Malthusians" believed that food production wasn't keeping up with the growth of population. They began a movement to limit the world's population. This was all before any modern farm equipment came in to use and before the reaper had even been invented.

Sir Thomas Gaulton, a cousin of Darwin, wrote a book named "Hereditary Genius" in1869, which presented the belief that talent and intelligence is inherited and he coined the word,"Eugenic", meaning "good genes". Those of lower classes or races were deemed "Disgenic" or possessing "bad genes". This gave more impetus to the Malthusian's goal.

Many prominent people such as, Teddy Roosevelt, George Bernard Shaw, H.G. Wells, Hellen Keller, (of all people), Winston Churchill, Alexander Graham Bell, and Margeret Sanger the founder of Planned Parenthood all preached this nonsense. Planned Parenthood has been the most successful Eugenics organization which has promoted population control based on race and is responsible for millions of abortions throughout the world. Sanger's "Birth Control Review" published articles by the Nazi Eugenicist, Dr. Ernst Rudin who was instrumental in Hitler's plan for racial cleansing.

The obvious intent of these people is shown in Sanger's letter to Clarence Gamble, (of "Proctor and Gamble", another eugenicist and founder of "The Pathfinders"), proposing what they called "The Negro Project" which was designed to eliminate what they believed to be an "inferior race". A host of others were firm believers in this philosophy. It still has many followers although they have changed the names of many of thier organizations and are less vocal since the results of Hitler's commitment to it came to light.

In modern times "Think Tanks" like "The Club of Rome" have come up with another scheme to limit population. In the "First Global Revolution", published by The Club of Rome they state; *"In searching for a common enemy against which we can unite, we came up with the idea that pollution, the threat of global warming, water shortages and the like would fit the bill.*

In their totality and their interactions these phenomena do constitute a common threat which must be confronted by everyone together. But in designating these dangers as the enemy we fall into the trap, which we already warned our readers about, namely mistaking symptoms for causes.

All these dangers are caused by human interference in natural pro-

cesses and it is only through changed attitudes and behavior that they can be overcome. The real enemy, then, is humanity itself...we believe humanity needs a common motivation, namely a common adversary in order to realize world government. It does not matter if this common enemy is a real one or one invented for the purpose."

This shows the intentions of these elitists to bring about a "New World Order" through population control and "Junk Science" all aimed at Globalism; a one world socialist government. The Club of Rome also believes that Democracy is a failure and a thing of the past due to political parties jockeying for power.

These people fall victim to the ridiculous idea that a Heaven on Earth can be brought about by proper management and reason depending on careful scientific analysis. They simply don't realize that they cannot cure mankinds struggles with pain, suffering, heartbreak, loss and disappointments through science, social engeneering, or political movements. In thinking that they can bring about a perfect world they fall for the words of the Serpent in The Garden, " Ye shall be like gods".

For eugenicists, people considered "Normal" were of Western Europian ancestry without any physical or mental disabilities. There were laws passed in many countries restricting marriages and isolating those deemed "Disgenic". Some eugenicists called for sterilization and many were subjected to this simply because they were poor or weren't intellegent enough or had an unacceptable family background. Some including George Bernard Shaw called for elimination of those whom were deemed unnecessary. He suggested gas as the most "humane" way.

While some countries had their solutions, and others made suggestions on how to keep the race pure, Hitler took it to the extreme and had just the kind of people around him to see it through. First they started with those that were mentally or physically disabled such as people with Downs syndrome, Cerebral Palsy and the feeble minded. They simply put them in the back of trucks and attached the exhaust pipe to the box with a hose and let the truck idle. Later they would develop more reliable, convenient and economically sound ways in special camps to do their evil act as the list of those found to be disgenic grew to just about anyone who was not officially recognized as Aryan.

When they would round up the Jews and Slavs of a conquered country it was announced that they were being relocated to the newly acquired territories. They were heading not for relocation; they were on a one way trip to the death camps. There were laws forbidding marriage or relations between Aryans and Jews. A law was passed that all Jews had to wear a yellow Star of David armband so they could be recognized and discriminated against. Eventually the people were worked up into an anti-Semitic frenzy which led to a night of breaking windows and burning Synagoges known as "Christalnaght". Most of the Jews in Germany and it's conquered countries were finally "relocated".

At first, to the western democracies these fascist countries and communist Russia seemed to be doing well economically while the rest of the world was in a depression. Other European nations began to turn to strong leaders to end the rioting and rebellion instigated by communists and anarchists. In Spain Franco came to power after a bloody civil war between communists and nationalists.

In 1931 King Alfonso XIII was deposed and a republican government was set up. This would seem in line with democratic principles and the rights of a people to govern themselves, but unlike the romantic tales woven by liberal writers, some of whom volunteered to fight on the Republican side, the government was nothing like what most people would call a Democratic Republic. The Republican side was made up of left leaning republicans and Freemasons in a coalition with anarchists and communists.

Less than a month after the Republic was proclaimed Catholic churches and establishments in Madrid, Sevilla and other cities were burned down. One scholar described the Republics constitution as the most hostile to religion in the 20th century. Historian Vicente Carcel Orti said that anticlerical Freemasons were instumental in bringing about anti-Catholic acts of the government. Freemasons held key government positions and had 183 deputies in parliament. Abilia Arroyo de Roman declared at a rally in the Salamancan pueblo of Macotera in 1933 that Spain was governed by Masonic lodges, intent on "decatholiciz-ing"'Spain, and the *Gaceta Regional* blamed the Law of Congregations on 'an occult power' that had taken refuge in Spain "to carry out its experiments".

The government showed all the signs of a communist government which has to include a war on the Catholic Church. Marx's idea of communism is based on atheism and a disregard for the individual personhood of mankind. This is directly opposed to what The Church stands for. For Marxist communism to be in any way affective the Catholic Church has to go.

Changes came about in the government and in private and public life as well. The legislative branch was changed to a single chamber called the Congress of Deputies. The constitution called for the nationalization of public services, land, banks, and railways. What came to be called "The Red Terror" spread throughout areas controlled by the government. Priests, bishops and anyone having anything to do with the Catholic church were sometimes killed on the spot without any legalities whatsoever.

In one particular show of ant-Catholicism a firing squad of communist militiamen "executed the Sacred Heart of Jesus" when it shot at a large statue of Jesus at Cerro de los Ángeles near Madrid, on 7 August 1936. The photograph published in the British Daily Mail showed what was the most infamous of the widespread desecration of religious property. Thousands of priests bishops and nuns were killed and Churches and Church property were torched. Murder squads, many times run by members of the Russian NKVD, (the forerunners of the KGB), were good at tracking down any Republicans that they may deem as "heritics" to communism.

With new elections, the Republicans won a victory and this gave rise to radicals calling for a complete revolution. Murders of the clergy and church burnings grew. Twelve bishops, 283 religious sisters and nuns; 4,184 priests; 2,365 religious priests; and an unknown number of laypeople were killed for their faith. People were asking when the army would step in and bring some sort of order. Finally the army across the Strait of Gibralter in North Africa's Spanish Moroco rose up under the command of Generalissimo Francisco Franco. The Spanish Civil War was on.

Stalin's Soviet Union as well as Lazaro Cardenas' leftist leaning Mexican government and many communists, socialists and liberals from Europe and the Americas gave aid to the communist Republicans. Hitler and Mussolini came to the aid of the fascist Nationalists under Franco. What came about was a "proxy war" between fascism and communism. Franco had the support of most Catholics and conservative groups loyal to the monarchy. Most of the European and American nations did not approve of the new Spanish government especially since its only major ally was the Soviet Union.

The atrocities on both sides were terrible, but the Nationalists killed more in their desire to purge whole areas of communist influence and vengence for the atrocities committed against the clergy and the Catholic Church. In the end the nationalists under Franco were victorious. Both communist Russia and fascist Germany and Italy had each gained valuable combat experience. Within a short time Hitler and Stalin would sign a non-agression pact and invade Poland. Another example of "Diplomacy."

In England, King Edward was forced to abdicate the throne in order to marry an American socialite divorcee which was forbidden under the Church of England law. She was waiting on the divorce of her second husband and was considered unsuitable to be the Queen Consort. Since the King is the head of the church he is forbidden to marry a divorcee while her husband is still alive. Edward and his new wife were bitter over the situation. They were showing signs of being Nazi sympathizers and there were fears that he may join in on some German scheme and want to reclaim the throne.

The day after he abdicated he went to Austria. Later he married Mrs. Simpson in France and then went to Germany in October 1937 against the advice of the British government, and met with Hitler. The German media made the most of this propaganda treat as the Duke and Duchess gave full Nazi salutes during their visit.

After the outbreak of the war Edward was assigned to the British Military Mission in France. There were claims that Edward had leaked the plans for the defence of Belgium. When Germany invaded France in May 1940, the Duke and Duchess fled to Portugal, a neutral country. Lord Caldacott told Churchill that the Duke ,"is well known to be pro-Nazi and may become a centre of intrigue". Churchill threatened the Duke with a court-martial if he did not return to British soil.

Edward was appointed Governor of the Bahamas. He reportedly told an acquaintance, "After the war is over and Hitler will crush the Americans ... we'll take over ... They (the British) don't want me as their king, but I'll be back as their leader." He was reported as saying that, "It would be a tragic thing for the world if Hitler was overthrown". Besides Chamberlain's desire for appeasement before the war, there were many people in high places in England that wished to make peace terms with Hitler after the war had started.

Even in the United States the situation was getting dangerous. World War veterans were given certificates in 1924 for promised "Bonus" money to be paid out in 1945. Now it was the 30's and it was the depth of the depression and the veterans couldn't wait that long. They were desperate and needed money. They converged on Washington D.C. in what was called "The Bonus Army", set up a shantytown, and planned on staying there until the government gave in.

The police arrived, the marchers resisted and two of them were shot by the police and later died. The Army was called in and under Gen. McArthur, who believed it was a communist uprising, uprooted and drove out the veterans using tanks and gas and burned their shanties and belongings against the orders of President Hoover. One of the veterans wives miscarried and a 12 week old baby died in the hospital after the gas attack.

Shortly after the election of Franklin Roosevelt he issued an executive order that confiscated all monetary gold from the public and took America off the gold standard. There were several reasons he did this but what set the big bankers and industrialists off was the move to revalue gold from just over $20 per ounce to $35 per ounce. This was meant to incentivize foreign investors to export their gold to America, while also devaluing the U.S. dollar in an attempt to spark inflation. His executive order was later passed as the Gold Reserve Act.

Some American industrialists who dreaded communism began a plot to take over the government. They viewed FDR as too socialistic and some thought he was a communist so they connived with leaders of the American Legion to replace him. This is known as "The Business Plot" or "White House Plot". It is one of the most important events in American History, but hardly anyone has ever heard of it because of the powerful people involved. The very fabric of the United States was at stake and they have been able to keep this attempted coup from the public to this day because of the hold they had and still have, on the press, and politicians.

In 1933 two men approached retired Major General Smedley Butler who was a nationally respected advocate for veterans with a proposal that at first he found hard to believe. Butler was one of a special breed of "Old Corps" Marines and was the recipient of the Congressional Medal of Honor not once, but twice. He spoke out forcefully about the attack on the veteran's shanty town, criticizing former military colleagues and the Hoover administration.

Despite his open opposition to big business and banks, they felt they could appeal to him through the cover of veteran's needs and his duty for the good of the country since Roosevelt was leading the nation toward communism. Their plan was to raise an army of 500,000 men from the American Legion, armed by Remington Firearms. Then they would offer Roosevelt an ultimatum where he would relinquish power due to failing health and name Butler as the head of a newly created Cabinet post, "Secretary of General Affairs", to run the government. FDR would be basically a figurehead and Butler would become in effect a dictator; the American "Furor". Of course, he would be carrying out the wishes of the businessmen and the bankers as well.

Those who first approached Butler with the plot were Gerald MacGuire and Robert Clark who assured Butler that their cover story of the President being in bad health would work. McGuire told him, "You know the American people will swallow that. We have got the newspapers. We will start a campaign that the President's health is failing. Everyone can tell that by looking at him, and the dumb American people will fall for it in a second..." The businessmen also promised as much money as would be needed.

MacGuire was unabashedly candid to Paul French, a reporter whom General Butler trusted and had gone to with the story for collaboration. French pretended to be an anti-Roosevelt reporter and MacGuire told him, "We need a fascist government in this country... to save the nation from the communists who want to tear it down and wreck all that we have built in America. The only men who have the patriotism to do it are the soldiers, and Smedley Butler is the ideal leader. He could organize a million men overnight."

MacGuire had traveled to Italy to study Mussolini's fascist state, and came away impressed. He wrote glowing reports back to Robert Clark, suggesting that they implement the same form of government. MacGuire wrote Clark and Clark's attorney a letter describing the Croix-de-Feu, a fascist leaning French World War veterans organization with suggestions for the same type of organization in America.

It is hard for us to realize how so many people, especially businessmen admired Mussolini and Hitler in those early years before the atrocities became known. Many people on both sides of the ocean viewed them as a stabilizing factor in a turbulent world with communists and anarchists creating labor unrest and social upheaval. Many American companies were involved and had trade with Nazi Germany just as we have relations and trade with fascist and communist countries now even though we know the crimes against humanity that they commit. As Bob Dylan said, "Money doesn't talk; it swears".

The businessmen and bankers had overlooked the fact that although Butler was not happy with the state of affairs in the country, especially for the veterans, he had taken an oath to protect and defend the Constitution against all enemies both foreign and domestic. He went to Congress and reported the whole affair.

They opened hearings in the House of Representatives known as the McCormack–Dickstein Committee but the only one they called was McGuire and he denied the whole affair. None of the industrialists, businessmen, bankers nor military named was ever called. The New York Times wrote it off as a giant hoax and suggestions were made that Gen. Butler had taken leave of his senses.

Given the power that these men wielded and the fact that they even thought they could pull off such a coup, it's easy to see how the whole affair could be just set aside since politicians and news media are easily bought and sold. Smedley Butler was not one to be taken lightly and a man who served his country with such honor and bravery should be believed above industrialists and bankers that have no allegiance to any nation.

The committees report stated:

This committee has had no evidence before it that would in the slightest degree warrant calling before it such men as John W. Davis, Gen. Hugh Johnson, General Harbord, Thomas W. Lamont, Admiral Sims, or Hanford MacNider.

The committee will not take cognizance of names brought into the testimony which constitute mere hearsay.

This committee is not concerned with premature newspaper accounts especially when given and published prior to the taking of the testimony.

As the result of information which has been in possession of this committee for some time, it was decided to hear the story of Maj. Gen. Smedley D. Butler and such others as might have knowledge germane to the issue. ...

The Congressional committee final report said:

In the last few weeks of the committee's official life it received evidence showing that certain persons had made an attempt to establish a fascist organization in this country. No evidence was presented and this committee had none to show a connection between this effort and any fascist activity of any European country. There is no question that these attempts were discussed, were planned, and might have been placed in execution when and if the financial backers deemed it expedient.

This committee received evidence from Maj. Gen Smedley D. Butler (retired), twice decorated by the Congress of the United States. He testified before the committee as to conversations with one Gerald C. MacGuire in which the latter is alleged to have suggested the formation of a fascist army under the leadership of General Butler.

MacGuire denied these allegations under oath, but your committee was able to verify all the pertinent statements made by General Butler, with the exception of the direct statement suggesting the creation of the organization. This, however, was corroborated in the correspondence of MacGuire with his principal, Robert Sterling Clark, of New York City, while MacGuire was abroad studying the various forms of veterans organizations of Fascist character.

End of report.

Nothing ever came of the affair and to this day it is hardly known. McGuire died shortly afterward in a New Haven hospital of what was listed as pneumonia brought on by pressure over the affair. He was thirty seven. Samuel Dickstein who was a representative from New York for 22 years and went on to become a New York State Supreme Court justice was later exposed after the fall of the U.S.S.R. as being on the Soviet payroll for years as an agent of the NKVD/KGB. He was so unscrupulous that his code name was "Crook". It makes one wonder how many other politicians were on the Russian payroll.

The McCormack–Dickstein Committee went on to become The House Un-American Activities Committee which exposed many communists working within the government. These hearings had nothing to do with Joseph McCarthy and his hearings since he was a Senator. Later Gen. Butler became a noted speaker against capitalism and war. He felt that as a Marine he had done the dirty work for big business throughout Latin America and Asia. He wrote a short but stunning book in 1935 entitled, "War Is a Racket".

So at that time there was a man who had barely made a living in Vienna, sleeping in flop houses and selling his drawings in taverns and on the street. He joined the German army and fought in WWI. After The War he was sent by his superiors to infiltrate a political party. He left the army and became the leader of that party. He eventually took over the government and in effect infiltrated the army with the party he was supposed to infiltrate and had the entire German military swear an oath of loyalty to him personally. Then he went on to annex his homeland, Austria, and entered Vienna as a conquering hero with thousands lining his way waving Nazi flags. He was on the cover of Time magazine as man of the year for 1938.

Unknown to the world a man that few had ever heard of revealed a plot that would have made the U.S. a fascist state and probable ally of Germany. Bismark once said, "The Americans are very lucky people. They're bordered to the north and the south by weak neighbors and to the east and west by fish". Technology hadn't reached the point where the U.S. could be reached.

In the coming horrors of WWII America is universally recognized as "The Arsenal of Democracy". Without the industrial and military might of the United States the Allies would have been unable to defeat the combined fascist nations and imperialist Japan. Smedley Butler saved Democracy for America and indirectly for the whole world. If the "Business Plot" had succeeded and America had become a fascist country, then to Lincoln's bane, "government of the people, by the people, and for the people", would have perished from the Earth.

THE PLAYERS

Georg Hogel

Georg was 18 when he joined the Kriegsmarine in 1937. Before he could read he was fascinated by the pictures in the books his grandfather had of ships and U-boats in "The Great War". Later he read everything he could about the navy and he was especially drawn to U-boats. All ships can submerge, but only submarines can surface.

He had an uncle and a cousin who were in the navy during the war. The Kriegsmarine offered a 2 year enlistment for Funkmaat or radioman on U-boats instead of the 4 or 5 years that were required in the army. He was a licensed telegrapher and he enlisted to serve on the U-boats. He and his family planned that he would do his 2 years and then return to his home in Munich to start a small business with them. They had no idea that their plans would be postponed much longer than they thought.

Georg's adventurous dreams were soon shaken when he experienced life aboard a U-boat. It takes a very special man to be a sub-mariner and be able to withstand the conditions both in and out of battle. First of all a man could not in any way be claustrophobic. He would have to be able to hold together under extreme pressure. There were few things more terrifying in life than being in a submarine while under a depth charge attack. A sub-mariner had to be gregarious as well since the living quarters were tight and tempers could easily flare.

Living conditions aboard a German U-boat were worse than those on any other vessel. Each patrol could take anywhere from a few weeks to six months. The crew couldn't bathe or shave. They had to wear whatever clothes were on their backs with only one change of underwear and socks. There was foul weather gear to be worn on watch but it would always be soaking wet from the huge waves that would come crashing over the conning tower. Water was strictly rationed for drinking only and was especially low if one of the water tanks had to be filled with diesel if the patrol was to be long one without any contact with a "Milchkuh" (milk cow) or a sub-tender. A "Milchkuh" was U-boat specially fitted to re-supply other U-boats at sea.

At the beginning of a patrol as much food as possible was crammed into every available place in the boat. One of the two toilets would be filled to the overhead with food. This toilet couldn't be used untill the food was eaten. Hams and sausages and other various foodstuff would be hung from pipes and supports and after a few days would take on an oily taste. They brought the best foods available with them, fresh meat, sausages, bread, fresh fruits and vegetables, but with the small refrigerators the food spoilt quickly; then the diet consisted mainly of canned goods. They also ate a soy based filler called Bratlingspulver that was is-sued for U-boat crews. They called it "diesel food", because of the constant exposure of diesel exhaust that surrounded them.

War was looming since Hitler had marched his troops into Czechoslovakia. Three times before Sept of 1939 the U-boats were sent on station to intercept any Allied ships only to be re-called as tensions died down. Georg was on leave when the tele-gram came ordering him to return to Wilhemshaven. He and his family felt that the war was about to begin. He was assigned to U-30 a Type VIIA ocean going U-boat. Her captain was Oberleu-tenant Fritz Julius Lemp. He would be with him until the end.

Thurs Malm

Nineteen year old Thurs Malm was an ordinary seaman on board the Swedish freighter MS Canton as she made her way along the west coast of Ireland en route to Liverpool. He and his cousin, Halga were longing to go to sea and so they went to Gothenburg 2 days after Christmas of 1938. Like so many young men they were looking forward to adventure and seeing the world. Just before New Years Day he signed on to MS Canton and Halga signed on to the MS Tunaholm a ship from the same company, Brostromes.

Sweden found itself in a precarious situation during the war. While remaining neutral her coastal vessels supplied Germany with the iron ore and steel Hitler needed and her ocean going ships were mostly involved with supplying the Allies. German blockades kept them as isolated from the Allies as possible but they still managed to support the Norwegian resistance. Sweden was also a refuge for any anti fascists and a haven for Jews.

Thurs was settled in his berth on the Canton. He had enjoyed his trip to the exotic Far East. For him it was an adventurous oriental cruise to "far away places with strange sounding names". His stay in India and the stops along the way were intriguing to a young man from a small town in Sweden. He couldn't wait to get home to family and friends and tell of the mysterious places he had been and the strange things he had seen. Now he was in for the greatest adventure in his life; one that he would never forget.

M.S. Canton had left Calcutta with a load of pig iron, linseed, and general cargo. She made a short stop at Freetown on the West Coast of Africa. They were hoping to avoid the U-boats that were lurking in the Celtic and Irish Seas and the approaches to the English Channel as she made her way around the west of Ireland. They planned on entering the Irish Sea from the north where they could have protection from Northern Ireland on one side and Scotland on the other. As they neared Tory Island off the coast of Donegal they had no idea that they were being watched. U-30 was on the prowl.

Fritz Julius Lemp

Fritz Julius Lemp was an enigmatic man as so many ambitious young men are apt to be. The word "Enigma" plays an ironic part in his fate. He was born in Tsingtau China on Feb. 19th, 1913, the son of a German officer assigned to the German legation in an area that had been leased from China. At the beginning of World War I his father brought the family back to Germany before the Japanese took the city in 1914. Little is known about his youth in Germany but he joined the German Navy, (Kriegsmarine), in 1931 when he was eighteen. By the time the war started he was in command of U-30 which was a Type VIIA submarine; the principal sea going U-Boat used at the time. He was 25.

His career started off on somewhat of a wrong footing when U-30 was involved in a collision with another U-boat during a submerged training exercise. The cause was unclear but Lemp showed considerable courage and ability by getting all of his men to safety. Some of his exploits seem almost comical. He is known to have fired the first "shot" of the war with the sinking of the Athenia, but earlier on the first day U-30 fired the first torpedo of the war at a rock which they thought was a cruiser. There was no entry in the log of whether the rock was sunk or not.

On their second cruise when he stopped the Fannet Head, a British ship, he found himself being pounded by Aircraft and destroyers that nearly sunk the boat. He hadn't anticipated that the ship's radio man had gotten off a signal before the crew was allowed to abandon ship. It stating they had been stopped by a German U-boat and gave the position. Lemp had sent a boarding party to the ship to look for bread which the U-boat was sorely in need of and a line was attached to a dinghy to transport the boarding party and any supplies they found. The Arc Royal an aircraft carrier with its escorts was not far off and before Lemp knew it there were Swordfish biplanes diving on them with bombs.

This in itself was a debacle since the first plane flown by an inexperienced pilot flew too low when he dropped his bombs and the blast damaged the bottom of the fuselage and the plane crashed with the pilot and gunner in the water. The second plane made the same mistake and now there were four airmen in the water. The third thought the wreckage and the churned up water below him was from the U-boat and dropped his bombs on his own men killing two and badly wounding the other two. They managed to make it to the Fannet Head and were taken on board by the German boarding party.

After diving and maneuvering he realized the dinghy still attached was marking his position. He surfaced and one of the crew with a knife in his teeth like a pirate cut the line and they submerged. When he surfaced again after the planes had left and brought the boarding party and wounded British airmen aboard he finally torpedoed the Fannet Head. He then watched the ship split in two and go down revealing two destroyers bearing down hard on them which they couldn't see from the other side of ship.

"ALARM" was the call as they dove and then were subject to over six hours of depth charges. The pipes were popping, spouting water and they had to spend a lot of time and effort bailing and pumping it out. Many of the instruments faces cracked and were dysfunctional. They endured this and then finally when it seemed to be quiet they had to surface for lack of air and need to recharge their batteries. The seas were heavy and the destroyers were gone.

They received orders to sail for Iceland and leave the most seriously wounded there for medical care. After two days of sailing they ended out right back where they had sunk the Fannet Head. Their magnetic compass was malfunctioning after the depth charge attack and they had sailed around in a wide circle. They had engaged the Fannet Head on the 14th of September and it was on the 19th of September when they sailed into Reykjavik.

One of the British airmen was in very bad shape by this time and he and one of the U-boatmen were taken ashore first. The rest of the wounded were taken ashore as soon as possible. Iceland was neutral and they had no facilities for prisoners of war so the Germans were assigned to embassy duty after promising not to try to escape. Later on the Americans took over Iceland and they spent the rest of the war in POW camps.

When U-30 returned to Wilhemshaven two distinguished guests came aboard. First was Adolph Hitler himself who shook Lemps hand, commended the crew and talked loudly about getting their wounded shipmates back from Iceland. The next visitor was Admiral Karl Dönitz, Chief of the U-Bootwaffe. He liked Lemp and helped him out of some of the trouble he was in for sinking the Athenia.

Lemp went on to become one of the U-boat aces; sinking 17 ships while captain of U-30. Due to the tight living conditions and the relative size of a U-boat, the crews were usually very close and rank and discipline was much more lax than in the other branches of the military. As long as these men kept sinking allied tonnage the Reich was willing to overlook any lack of decorum that wouldn't be tolerated in the Wiermacht. After all they sailed out in what was called "floating coffins" and a little slack was due such men.

Lemp made eight cruises in U-30 and had an especially successful one in the summer of 1940. He sank six ships as well as torpedoing and slightly damaging the British battleship HMS Barham killing four sailers and wounding two others.

Donitz awarded him the Knight's Cross of the Iron Cross which was the highest award Germany had. It was given only to those showing extreme bravery and leadership in battle. He was well liked by his men, and had little regard for spit and polish but still was clearly in command. The Cross was held in high regard and his men were proud to serve under him. His crew made one for him in the machine shop when they received the news of his award at sea. He was the archetypal German U-Boat skipper; young, good looking and more than a bit arrogant.

Jim McLoughlin

My father was born and raised in poverty. In the area we came from in the west of Ireland very few people could be called wealthy. Of course there were the landlords who were mostly English or Anglo Irish for whom many worked either directly or indirectly. They would hire some people as day laborers, and some as permanent workers. They owned vast tracts of land and would charge rent to the small farmers to live and work on the land in a very similar fashion to how it had been for ages.

He was born in 1909, and therefore a British subject. He would have to stand aside as a boy and doff his cap with the rest of the men as one of the "upper class" would go by in their fine carriages. As a child, he and his older brother, John, had to go off early in the morning to work rather than to school. They would walk the icy roads in winter holding on to each other to keep from falling or plod along in the frequent rain to earn a little money for the family.

His education went as far as the third grade. Yet he was able to read, write, and cipher well enough to get through the rest of his life, always keeping well informed about the world around him. He didn't have much of a formal education, but he was smart, and quick to learn. He developed skills that were needed and he was able to help put money and food on the table for the family.

He was the second of eight children. One of his brothers, Francis died at just two and half years old. This was the case with just about all the families in those days in that area. Infant and child mortality was high. My father helped build the coffin for his brother when he was a child and later as a man made the headstone, which is still there in the small cemetery of the ruins of Saint Cummin's chapel which gives its name to Kilcummin meaning Cummin's Church.

My father was a hard working fisherman farmer as were most of the people of the coast. He was one of a dying race of European Peasants that were the backbone of western civilization. Like so many people in rural areas he was pretty much a jack of all trades. When they needed something done they couldn't just call someone to do it for them. They had no phones, no electricity, no automobiles. They had to do whatever needed to be done themselves or have a friend or relative to help.

Jim was talented in various skills. He was a good carpenter, making anything from a fiddle, to a boat; a cartwheel to a spinning wheel. Being a stone mason as well, he built and repaired houses; mostly your typical whitewashed cottages that are so much a part of Ireland's landscape.

When he was just a boy he began fishing with his father and meeting the ships that would enter the bay to sail up the Moy River to Ballina. My grandfather and some of the local men were pilots who would be taken on to bring the ships up the tricky river. The first deck my father set foot on was a Swedish four masted sailing ship that brought timber from Scandinavia to Ballina and returned with sea stones for ballast. The sailors hoisted him aboard and gave him something to eat and some chocolate as well. He met the captain who sported long sideburns, wore a blue greatcoat with double breasted brass buttons and looked every bit the part of the bygone days of wooden ships and iron men.

He became a pilot at 19 and longed to go to sea. But as an important provider for his family, as well as the love he had for his home, he pleased himself with bringing the big ships up the river and fishing as well as helping tend the family farm. He had the knack of being content and thankful for what he had and the confidence to know that if there was work to be done he was quite capable of doing it. What he preferred most of all was fishing since one of his great loves was the sea.

He was thirty-one that summer of 1940, and the fishing had been "fair to middlin" as they would say. He owned a 22-foot open skiff he named the St. Anne. He fished with her along with seven other men one of whom was his brother Mike. They were all close friends and some related to each other, as are so many people in rural places. Just about everyone is someone's cousin.

The trim little blue and white boat had put quite a few "bob" in their pockets and kept dinners on their tables as well. She was a lucky boat, light and maneuverable and as he told me, "she sailed on the water not in it." The sinewy arms of these men of the sea provided her power. None of them could swim a stroke. The water is too cold and wild, and so very few people ever learned. They viewed it as only putting off the inevitable if you were unlucky enough to fall out of a boat and so the emphasis was on not falling out of a boat. This made these fishing folk very good seamen in all kinds of weather.

With the small piece of land that his large family owned they were able to keep body and soul together but the letter or package from America was always more than welcome. Most of the people had at least one or two family members in America or England and as hard pressed as they were themselves to scrape out a living in their new homes they would always send a little something back to the family. Sometimes it was no more than some old clothes that were old when they themselves got them, but Ireland was a very poor country and the people were in need.

Once as my father and I were out driving in Ireland during the 80's he had me pull over along a road that ran through an old abandoned village. It was like many others I had seen in Ireland and I had assumed they were pretty ancient presumably destroyed during one of the many wars as was the ruined monasteries from the time of Cromwell.

They were just roofless stone walls covered with lichen and vines, but the old man scanned the sight before him with watery eyes and told me of how he remembered the good times he had visiting friends and playing cards and being at dances in that forgotten village. I asked him what had happened to the people and why the village was abandoned. His answer consisted of two letters, - "TB". He told me that Tuberculosis had wiped them out. "TB killed them", he sighed. There was a pause as I looked about and then I turned and said to him, "No, Dad, poverty killed them."

THE EYE OF THE STORM

The Republic of Ireland, comprising 26 counties of the small island, was neutral. Six counties of the province of Ulster were part of the British Empire and at war with Germany. Many British ships were built in Belfast and it was a vital part of the war effort. Germany blitzed the North of Ireland as it did England. They inadvertently dropped bombs on a few occasions in the Republic, killing several and causing much damage. Apologies from Germany were accepted and after the war West Germany paid Ireland retribution for the death and destruction caused. The money came from funds provided by the Martial Plan which meant that the American taxpayers paid for damages done by Germany to a neutral country.

Each side hoped for the Republic to join them and Germany had high hopes since it knew well the bad blood that still existed due to the age old struggle of the Irish to free themselves of England's rule. With Hitler occupying France on one side and the possibility of a German allied Ireland on the other, England would be choked into submission.

Germany had helped the rebel cause and the "Easter Rising" in 1916 by smuggling guns to aid the insurrection, which eventually brought about the Republic. But despite the bitter feelings toward England for their long and cruel treatment there were too many social, linguistic and economic ties for Ireland to cast in its lot with the Nazis after finally winning their independence. They were not about to trade one Germanic oppressor for another. Besides strong family ties with England and America there were cultural bonds that just didn't exist with the Germans. And so DeValara, the president of the Republic wisely chose to stay neutral just as other European nations had. Eamon DeValara was born in Brooklyn.

He declared a state of "Emergency" and let the world know that Ireland intended to be neutral, but top secret information that was declassified and released in the 1970's show that in some cases they weren't as "neutral" as they claimed.

The Irish Air Force and the RAF joined together in finding bases in Ireland for a possible "Doomsday" scenario where one or the other island might be invaded by the Nazis. Any downed German pilots that were captured were kept in prison camps and treated harshly at first, but later were allowed to have leave in the community. British prisoners were quietly repatriated or allowed to escape to Northern Ireland. About five thousand soldiers in the Irish Army deserted and went off to fight for the Allies.

The most secret aid given the Allies was permission to set up a weather station on an island in Black Sod Bay on the west coast of Mayo. This station was vital in keeping track of the weather and was especially instrumental in giving up to the minute reports to Eisenhower as he anxiously awaited a break in the terrible weather they were having in the Channel in early June of 1944. A break in the weather was immediately reported and the D-Day landing went forward on the 6th[th].

The West Coast of Ireland had seen more than its share of shipwrecks over the years. The Spanish Armada met its final end in 1588 in one of the many gales that are common in that wild part of the North Atlantic. Down through the ages men of that area have put to sea plying their trade as fishermen and seafarers in all kinds of weather both fair and foul.

To the North West in County Mayo there is a large bay named Killala for the ancient town it washes and gives some shelter facing just about due north. The wind and waves can be treacherous in those seas and the rocky irregular shoreline has many small inlets. Kilcummin Head is at its northern end separating the bay from Lacken Strand. This is a vast beach of over 600 acres of strand and 500 acres of marshland. Most of it is covered during high tide but has a "Channel" of water from the Cloonalaghan River when the tide is out.

On this stretch of sand would wash up much of the flotsam of the ships that were sunk in the battle of the Atlantic between the great world powers that were at war. That summer of 1940 the Republic of Ireland found itself in the eye of that tremendous storm and the little island was virtually untouched except for the wreckage that would wash up on its shores. The people, being very poor and in some cases destitute would glean what they could find. The great wooden beams that would wash up were especially valuable since wood was so expensive. The men would salvage them and for a fee would take them to the saw mill to be cut into lumber.

Being God fearing seafaring people they took no pleasure in the thoughts of what was happening far out at sea. The sinking of a ship is almost like the death of something alive. A once beautiful and useful craft sinking into a watery grave gives no right-minded person pleasure except for the enemy that sank it. The sight of personal belongings that once meant so much to someone being washed ashore is a melancholy one indeed.

Worst of all were the bodies of those who sailed those ships in various states of death and decay tossed about by the waves and lying in the sand amid the wreckage picked at by sea birds. These were not just so much flotsam. They were people who once breathed and laughed and cried. People who once loved and were loved and then violently died.

The bodies were treated with great respect and prayed over, and then they were taken away and sent off to England where they were returned to their families. My mother told of one such poor soul, which she particularly remembered. It stuck in her mind because she had seen the body of this unfortunate man as he lay on the beach and although he was in a very sad state what struck her most was the sleeve of his tattered uniform with the brass buttons lying empty on the sand. She went home crying and sick and according to her she "Didn't eat a bit for a week". The family came personally to retrieve their son's body.

The war was good for fishing and the Brits bought up just about everything that was edible. Even the wings from the skate, which were plentiful in those waters, found use as food for soldiers on the front, but there was something else that was plentiful in those waters as well; the dreaded U-boats.

They found the rough irregular coastline of Ireland a relatively safe haven. Ships were the lifeline to England and the Germans had been so successful at sinking them that the British newspapers stopped reporting the losses for fear of affecting the morale of the people. The "Blitz" was bad enough. England was in sad shape. She alone withstood the onslaught of Hitler's blitzkrieg. The rest of Europe was either fascist or communist or neutral, which would have been a short-lived position once England had fallen.

The U-Boats could take advantage of the many small inlets along the rough irregular coast and the fact that the Republic of Ireland had very little to speak of as a navy. They could lie submerged with snorkel and recharge their batteries and surface at night giving the crew much needed deck time and fresh air from the stifling stench below.

It was rumored that German sailors in civilian clothes were seen in clubs and bars in Dublin. Once they sailed in and docked at a pier in Kerry to drop off survivors of a Greek ship they had torpedoed. There were several reports of U-boat crews coming ashore to buy fresh vegetables that they were always lacking. These U-boatmen were audacious enough to come ashore in the most unlikely places. One night off the coast of Florida a mine was touched off by a German U-boat and in the morning among the wreckage washed up on the beach one of the bodies had a movie ticket from a local theater in his pocket.

My father and a friend were out fishing one day and saw what appeared to be a steel pipe sticking out of the water. They rowed over to see what it was in such a familiar place. When they took hold of the "pipe", and looked down, they saw what appeared to be the deck of a ship stretched out beneath them. They immediately blessed themselves and put foam on the water with their oars as they left the scene frightened at what they thought was a huge piece of a shipwreck. Wreckage didn't usually float into Killala Bay, it washed up on Lacken Strand on the other side of Kilcummin. What they probably saw was the snorkel and deck of a U-boat.

THE END OF THE CANTON

The Canton was cruising along on a calm summer sea near Tory Island west of Donegal. The crew was looking forward to reaching their destination. Liverpool is a thriving city on the West coast of England. It had been a seaport for centuries and there was plenty of entertainment for seamen after a long voyage. It was a bustling city with people from all over the world. The men knew that after they docked they would celebrate for a few days and then would be on their way back to Sweden after their long voyage. They were looking forward to some good times in Liverpool and then home to family and friends.

Lemp came upon the Canton at about 8:30 on the night of August 9th 1940. He spotted her in the half light silhouetted against the northern sky. He fired a single torpedo without stopping her and permitting the crew to abandon ship. Again he showed his enigmatic behavior. With some ships he went by the rules and with others he didn't. The Canton was unarmed and posed no threat. Three of the ships he had sunk were by mines he had laid so it's understandable in situations like that or when attacking a convoy that is escorted by warships. But why did he observe the rules with some unarmed merchant ships and then sink the Canton without warning?

Thurs had just come off watch, and was below in the galley having a cup of coffee. Suddenly there was a great explosion. The ship rolled and was shook from stem to stern. Thurs was knocked off his feet to the deck of the galley. He got up and made his way to the main deck. The hatches had been blown sky high landing in the sea about him. The ship was slightly rolling with the impact. He looked into number four hold and saw nothing but darkness but there was no water coming in yet. As he made his way to his lifeboat station on the starboard side he realized that he had forgotten his life vest. He ran back to his cabin, retrieved his life jacket and headed back to his boat station.

Fires were breaking out below decks. The ships horn was blaring hoping to attract another ship to come to their rescue. The lifeboat he was assigned to with the captain and 15 men sailed off and disappeared into the gloom. He ran to another boat that was being lowered. There was near panic on the deck as one of the men in haste cut the line too soon and sent some of the crew of the second lifeboat tumbling into the water. Thurs and the others found their way to another lifeboat and he and the remaining 15 men of the crew of the Canton shoved off from the stricken ship.

At those latitudes during the summer the Sun skirts below the horizon and it doesn't get very dark but more like twilight. Thurs looked back and after 20 minutes the afterdeck was below the water level as she lifted her forecastle at least 25 meters in the air and slipped beneath the waves stern first with the boilers blowing on the way down. For most of them all of their worldly possessions went down with the Canton. Now they were alone and virtually helpless on an unknown sea. The captain and the crew of the other lifeboat that Thurs was assigned to was never seen nor heard from again.

The ships carpenter was a good boatsman and the first night when the wind picked up and the seas became heavy he had them row into the wind. One of the men had propped himself in the stern and only muttered. He was obviously in shock. In the afternoon of the second day they sighted land. By now the seas were getting very heavy and the men were cold, wet, tired and afraid. The next morning they found themselves sailing eastward with the land on their right, too weak to row and driven by a gale toward the cliffs of Sligo.

THE RESCUE

J im was sitting down having his breakfast of tea, soda-bread and butter with his father and mother and his brothers Mike, George and Peter. There was no fishing that day. It was beautiful, bright and sunny, but a gale force wind was blowing with white caps on the ocean which kept the boats frapped down at the slip. The sea was too rough and it was a day for chores around their small farm and some time off.

News from the Coast Watchers had gone out and spread rapidly throughout the villages about a lifeboat that had been sighted and was heading past Kilcummin Head. The men choked down their bread and tea and went off up the fields to the cliffs of Crough Mor to see the sight. There were a few people there already and some of them had started saying the Rosary.

Jim looked on with fear for the boat he was watching far off in the distance. He knew well what was going to happen. The waves were huge and in tumult with white caps threatening death to anyone in a boat. There was really nothing that could be done. They would be smashed to pieces on the cliffs and that would be the end of them. Tragedy was not new to these people since they all had family and friends that had been lost at sea.

Jim realized that Willy Knox was standing by his side. Willy was a short stocky man who had known Jim all his life and was one of his fishing partners. They spoke a few words about the scene they were witnessing before them. As men of the sea they were caught up in the moment and all they could do was agree that the plight of the survivors was grim. They felt deep sorrow as well as helplessness.

Jim then slowly turned his head and looked at Willy with sort of a wistful semi-smile and that twinkle in his eye he often had, and said, "Will we try it?" Willy looked him right in that twinkling eye and said "Let's go"! Mike heard them and said he was game too. Their father thought they were daft, but he knew that if anyone could do it, it would be Jim. So off they went through the fields to the house and despite my grandmother's pleading, they set out for the slip.

The word went out about what was happening and the rest of the crew showed up ready to take their places in the boat. There were a few others on the scene and they took the fraps out from under the boat and set about launching her into the heavy rollers that were washing up on the cobblestone slip. Everyone took off their caps, blessed themselves and said a short silent prayer. With some difficulty they managed to set out. It was rough going but they got the nimble little boat about and headed out into the bay.

As they cleared the "storm wall" the wind picked up and they realized immediately this was more than they bargained for. The St. Anne was like a cork as she skimmed the water first in a deep trough and then atop the crest of a huge wave. They headed her into the wind and pulled the oars with all their might to keep her steady on some sort of course toward the lifeboat in the distance. All of them started to get worried and wondered if they had made the right decision. They had been through rough weather before but it came upon them at times when they were out fishing already. This was different. No one put to sea in such weather purposely.

The dread really started to hit home when they saw to their stern the steamer Tartar which was entering the bay on its way out from Ballina come about and head back up the River Moy for shelter because the seas were so bad in the bay. If it was too bad for a ship what was it like for a 22 ft boat? One of the men started grumbling that this was too much. "Ah, this is no good boys", he said. "Let's turn about and head back or we will all be lost!" But Willy Knox with courage way beyond his size threatened to "Split" him with the oar if he didn't shut up. They settled into pulling the oars as they were so used to doing as if they were a well oiled machine.

At times they lost sight of the lifeboat and could only go on dead reckoning as to which direction she might be. They were soaked with spray, lips salted, and the sea spilled over the gunnels as two of the men shipped oars and began to bail.

As they drew nearer they could keep her in sight and then realized just how big the lifeboat was in comparison to the St. Anne. She was almost twice the size of the skiff. They could see no movement on the boat just yellow oil cloths and they began to wonder if there was anyone on board or if they had risked their lives to come out to an empty boat. But the original report from the Coast Watchers said that there were survivors on board and so they weren't going back after all this without finding out for sure. The lifeboat had quite a bit of water in it as well and she was riding low.

The closer they got, the larger she became. As they drew nearer they reached a point where they realized that they would have to stand off just enough that the lifeboat wouldn't come down on them and finish the act instantly. One moment she was way above them and the next she was deep below.

Jim had them come about so the lifeboat was to their lee. They called out but received no answer nor was there any movement. They called out repeatedly and then they saw someone lift up the oil cloth and look out, but then lower the cloth and disappear from sight. They could see movement aboard. After several more attempts to make contact hoping they could get someone to take a line, it seemed like the end. What more could they do if they couldn't get these people to take a tow line?

Jim wasn't about to give up. He told the men what he was going to do and they tried to talk him out of it, but his mind was made up. He gave control over to Willie and then tied the line around his waist and told the men to shift their weight in the boat.

He then watched carefully for the right moment with one foot on the gunnel of the boat. If he jumped into the lifeboat as it was coming up and the St. Anne was going down he could break both of his legs, or worse. If he jumped when his boat was on the up-surge and the lifeboat going down he may be propelled into the sea. So he waited and watched for just the right moment and then leapt from the St. Anne into the lifeboat. He almost broke his shinbone against one of the thwarts, but he made it and he was alright.

The survivors slowly came out from under the yellow oil cloths and Jim saw that they were alive although none the better for exposure after two days at sea driven by a relentless wind. He made his way foreword avoiding stepping on anyone, secured the line around his waist to the bow cleat and then after signaling to his crew he went aft, tucked the tiller under his arm and looked at and rubbed his aching leg. He knew it would be alright and at that time he just thanked God that so far everything was going well.

The haul home was tough going for the rest of them. The much larger lifeboat had 17 people and a lot of water in it and they had to keep ahead enough at times so that she wouldn't bear down on them. They were cold, wet, and tired. It was a good bit of extra weight to pull with one less oarsman, but they had saved the lives of the survivors of the Canton and that made it all worthwhile. They felt elated that they were on their way home after accomplishing what they had set out to do.

It had taken a few hours for them to reach the lifeboat and return and as they approached "The Storm Wall" they could see quite a bit of movement on the shore and the cliffs above. When they launched the boat there were only a few people at the slip. Now the shore was alive with people! They never expected this. There were cars full of people as well as ass-carts and bicycles and those on foot and horseback from all over the region. The word had gone out far and wide of what these fishermen were attempting and everyone wanted to see the sight.

They were cheering and waving as the men headed in. There was no problem with them pulling both boats up on the cobblestones since everyone wanted to take part in this. The men of the St. Anne were spent, but the 16 men from the Canton couldn't even stand up or walk at first after being cramped in the lifeboat for so long. Thurs and the others fell to their knees and had to be linked along. One of the crew who was a Filipino fell on his knees, blessed himself and kissed the ground.

The sergeant of the police in Killala was there with a few other policemen. He brought the crew of the Canton a bottle of whiskey and they were taken to the nearest houses and given hot tea, food and cigarettes. Several of the survivors spoke English and were able to tell of their ordeal. They were showered with kindness and compassion for all they had been through.

The sergeant made his way through the crowd and went right up to Jim, whom he knew, grabbed hold of him and cleared the way to take him up to the local pub and general store. He wanted to be the first to buy him a drink. Jim and Mike stopped to hug and kiss their mother and father as they made their way up from the shore. The rest of the crew's family's were there as well and the porter and whiskey flowed lavishly at the Munnelly's pub that day.

Jim and his father and his brother Mike, made their way home along the narrow dirt road that led up to Parke from Clougher not as sure footed as they came down. They went to bed and in a short while everyone was faintly snoring. Jim lay awake for some time thinking of the events of the day. His mind was racing and he still felt the pitching and the rolling of the boats in the storm and found it uneasy as he lay in bed.

He thought and shuddered about his jumping into the lifeboat thinking, what on Earth brought him to do that? He wasn't particularly more courageous than the other men with him but he felt that as the skipper of the boat and after proposing the whole idea it was his place to do it especially after seeing there were still people alive. He knew he could never live with himself if he had turned away. He said his prayers and a special one in thanksgiving to God for bringing him and his crew and the survivors of the Canton safely to shore.

The rescue was included in the British reports of rescues at sea in and around Great Britain which mostly consisted of motorized fishing boats picking up the crews of downed aircraft and stating the monetary awards given for the amount of "petrol" used. It stated,-

Kilcummin, Co. Mayo.

"The Swedish motor ship Canton was torpedoed in the Atlantic, on the 9th August, 1940, seventy miles N.W. of Ireland, while bound from Calcutta to Liverpool. She had a crew of thirty two. One of her boats, with sixteen men in it, arrived near Kilcummin at 10 in the morning of the 11th August. A north-west wind was blowing at almost gale force; there was a very heavy sea; and the boat was in danger of being wrecked. Eight men put out in a rowing boat and at great risk to themselves, brought the Canton's boat through the dangerous currents to safety. – Rewards, 8 pounds"

THE AFTERMATH

Thurs came ashore at the slip in Clougher with only a T-shirt and dungarees. In a letter he wrote to my brother he said, "I have never been poorer". They were given medical attention and later they were taken to Dublin and were given new clothes and stayed for seven months at the Savoy Hotel before being sent off to Liverpool. There they boarded a Swedish ship, the Manchuria bound for Petsumo Finland. Their spirits were bright as they looked forward to going home after their ordeal. Little did they know it wasn't over yet.

After a few days they spotted a plane. It was a German plane and it came in for an attack. It swooped in and dropped bombs on them while strafing the ship with its guns. The plane left. The bombs had missed them. The crew and survivors knew they would be coming back. They decided to get into the lifeboats but found they had been damaged during the attack.

The plane came back again firing it's machine guns and dropping bombs but this time a large hole was blown in the hull above the water line and into the Machine Room. They pulled together and with much effort fixed it with concrete.

The next day they spotted another plane, but this time to their relief it was a British search and rescue plane and they were hoping for the best. As they entered Finnish waters they saw a ship approaching. It was a German destroyer and it signaled them to follow. They brought them to a port in northern Norway called Vardo. They stayed there for two weeks under constant German guard before they were ordered to sail down the coast of Norway to reach Gothenburg Sweden. After a week they stopped at Tromso for fresh water. They had another 24 hour guard on board and had to stay another week. Then they were ordered to turn around and go back to resume their voyage to Petsumo Finland.

At this point Thurs left the ship to make his own way home. He traveled over 400 kilometers in a Swedish truck over very bad dirt roads to Rovaniemi Finland. From there he took a train to his home in Sweden. Later he served in the Swedish navy, married a local girl and they had a son a daughter and three grandchildren. He eventually bought a fishing boat and spent the rest of his life fishing around his beloved home. His adventure was over and it was enough to last him a lifetime.

Oberleutenant Lemp, while captain of U-30 sank one other ship, the Clan MacPhee, a week after sinking the Canton. He was then ordered to return to Germany and given command of U-110 one of the newest class of U-boats. It was a type IXB. It was larger, faster and had a range of 12,000 nautical miles on the surface and 64 miles while submerged until needing to surface to recharge the batteries. They were proud of their new boat as well as their skipper. U-30 was assigned to use as a training vessel with half of the crew staying on as instructors and the other half including Georg Hogel shipping out with Lemp in the new boat. U-30 survived the war and eventually was scuttled by her crew rather than surrender her.

Unlike U-30, U-110 turned out to be an unlucky boat. They set out from Kiel in March of 1941 and came upon their first victim in convoy HX 112 on the 16th. He claimed that he damaged a freighter but there was no confirmation. The next ship he came upon was the British tanker Erodona south of Iceland. He claimed to have sunk her, which he didn't, but she did sustain some damage. He reported sinking an 8,000 ton tanker, but his torpedoes hit nothing and any explosions heard were probably from the torpedoes at the end of their run.

Just before dawn on the 23rd they attacked the Siremalm but the torpedo failed to detonate and left a large dent in the hull. The crew manned the 105mm deck gun but in the excitement neglected to remove the plug in the muzzle and the gun exploded seriously injuring three men. They then used the 37mm and 20mm guns and despite being hit several times the Siremalm successfully zigzagged away and escaped. U-110 had to cut the patrol short and put into Lorient for aid for the wounded and repairs due to the gun's explosion. Not a good start.

U-110 left Lorient on 15th of April 1941. She sank the Andra Moyrant near the Blasket Islands off the coast of Kerry. It was a 2,471 ton French freighter and not much of a prize but it brightened their hopes of a successful mission this time. After receiving news of a convoy rounding the southern tip of Iceland, Lemp raced to a rendezvous point to join up with other U-boats in a Wolf Pack.

On May 9th the U-boats converged on convoy OB 318. There were plenty of ships available, so much so that it would be hard to miss. This reminded them of the early days of the war which they called "The Good Times" when the U-boats roamed free sinking Allied shipping at will. There were plenty of ships, but unlike the "Good Times" they were well guarded by escorts.

At 11:48 he attacked. He fired a spread of 3 "eels' into the convoy and minutes later the British freighter Esmond blew up and was sinking. Another explosion sent the Bangor Head to the bottom. Lemp was elated, but his joy was short lived. By this time the Royal Navy had honed its skills at seeking and destroying U-boats and American Lend Lease destroyers helped to provide the extra ships needed. Convoy OB 318 was surrounded by corvettes and destroyers manned by highly trained crews and they were determined to protect the vitally needed ships.

Lemp again made a terrible mistake. After his initial success instead of diving he remained at periscope depth to watch the ships he had just torpedoed go down. A lookout from HMS Aubrieta, one of the corvettes, spotted his periscope and the warship went racing toward him at full speed.

"ALARM!" He dove hard but ten depth charges came raining down on them. Lemp ordered a deep dive and a 90 degree turn to starboard, but HMS Aubrieta's ASDIC operator was well trained and kept "pinging" U-110 wherever she went. Twenty minutes after the first attack the Aubrieta attacked again. More depth charges pounded U-110 springing leaks throughout the boat and sending her stern first down to 300 meters. Lemp gave the order to blow all ballast for her to surface. He announced; "Last stop, everybody off". The crew knew this meant abandon ship. HMS Bulldog and HMS Broadway, formally the USS Hunt joined the Aubrieta for the finish.

As the U-boat surfaced the guns of the three warships came to bear on her. Some of the Brits mistakenly thought they were going to man the deck gun. Fourteen of the submariners were cut down by machine gunfire and their lifeless bodies slid down the hull and into the dark water.

The captain of the Broadway headed straight for the U-boat to ram her. The rest of the German crew jumped for the relative safety of the sea. The skipper of the Broadway suddenly realized that she was abandoned and dead in the water and he opted instead to capture her. He ordered full astern and hove to with the helm hard a-starboard, but it was too late. The Broadway ripped open her port bow as she scraped against the U-boat's dive plane. She was also damaged below the water line amidships and her port propeller was shorn away. She had to stand off.

Sub-lieutenant David Balme led a party of eight in a launch from the Bulldog to board the U-boat. Lemp and the rest of the surviving crew were swimming in the water not too far off. They had pulled the sea cocks but the boat wasn't sinking. They hadn't bothered to set the scuttle charges as they thought she would sink or be rammed by HMS Broadway.

When Lemp realized that his boat would be boarded he began to swim back furiously. One of the officers, who was Lemp's cousin, tried to stop him and they struggled in the water for a while until Lemp broke free and continued swimming toward the U-boat. At this point just like so many other situations in Lemp's short career there is controversy over his demise. One version according to the Germans had it that he was shot by a sailor with a rifle from one of the ships. Another version says that he was shot by Balm as he tried to board the U-boat.

In my opinion I find both of these stories to be false. First of all the Brits were never known to purposely kill any survivors at sea and to shoot someone with a rifle from a pitching and rolling vessel is more luck than marksmanship. The Brits maintained the unwritten law of the sea, which is to rescue all survivors, without any wartime rules to guide them. Any seaman who would have taken such an action upon himself would face a court marshal. Besides that, what would be the benefit of shooting the captain of a vessel you were about to capture? It would have been impossible for him to stop nine armed men from doing whatever they wanted. Wouldn't he be of more value as a POW?

I tend to believe the account of Georg Hogel who stated that the survivors weren't really in a position to see what had happened and that Lemp had been sick and not feeling well at the time. He believed that the struggle with his cousin and the strain of swimming in icy cold waters were too much for him and his heart gave out. Balm stated that no shots were fired during the boarding and some of the Brits said they saw Lemp just throw his hands up and slip beneath the waves.

The reason for Lemp's frantic try to get back to the boat was because he didn't want the British to capture what was on it. He didn't want to die with the ignominy of loosing what was on board. It wasn't gold or precious jewels but something much more important that could only be measured in blood. In Georg's radio room were all his code books, ciphers, maps and charts and something else even more important that Lemp was willing to give his life for.

When the boarding party first saw it they thought it was some sort of strange typewriter. What they found was a top secret undamaged German code machine known as "Enigma". It was named "Enigma" by the Germans since they thought that the codes sent and received on it were unbreakable. It had a number of rotors as well as keys and the codes would be changed from time to time. It was a very complicated piece of machinery. Nobody knew what it was so they took everything with them.

The remaining survivors were taken aboard the Bulldog and U-110 was taken in tow to Scappa Flow but sank a short while later; or so they said. At Scappa Flow they were met by intelligence officers and cryptologist from Bletchley Park; a quiet out of the way English country estate that had been turned into headquarters for the efforts to break Germany's codes. The Poles had some success before the war and passed on information as well as smuggling out wooden copies of the Enigma machine to the Brits since many Poles were forced to work in the factories manufacturing them. But the Germans had refined it to a point where they couldn't keep up with the changes.

Now they had all they needed from U-110. With the captured code books, before long they were able to guide convoys and ships away from areas where the wolf packs were. In many cases as they progressed to break the Enigma code they were able to read messages before the German commanders received them. It was crucial that the Germans did not know they had broken the code.

The whole affair with U-110 was known as Operation Primrose and the fact that the code was broken was classified as "The Ultra Secret". Churchill didn't tell Roosevelt about the capture until

January of 1942. It's hard to overestimate the value of this find. June of 1941 saw Allied shipping losses at 432,000 tons. By August it was less than 80,000 tons.

The skipper of HMS Bulldog, Baker-Cresswell, was given the DSO, (Distinguished Service Order), and promoted to captain. King George VI told him that the capture of U-110 and the material aboard was, "the most important single event in the whole war at sea". "The Ultra Secret" was declassified in the 1970's and has changed the way historians view the War. Now we know that the Allies had a tremendous advantage over the Axis and it leaves one to realize the power of the enemy since it took another four years to defeat them.

Georg was in the water with the remaining crew of U-110. He was picked up by the Brits and spent the rest of the war in POW camps in England and Canada. After the war he was sent to the former Nazi death camp, Dachau which had been turned into a POW camp.

When the camp was liberated by the Americans the horrors of what had been going on in Nazi Germany were exposed. The G.I.'s who first arrived were so shocked, angered and disgusted at what they saw around them that they lined up an estimated fifty of the SS guards against a wall and executed them on the spot. Some they threw into the prisoner's barracks and let the inmates take care of them. Those that were shot were the lucky ones. The former SS guards that had survived the wrath of the G.I.'s were eventually kept in a separate area awaiting trial as war criminals. The rest of the German POW's were treated well; certainly better than the former inmates.

It took a long time to process prisoners as some of the SS and other war criminals were trying to pass as ordinary soldiers. Himler himself, the head of the SS, was spotted by a British officer as he tried to be repatriated wearing a soldiers uniform. When recognized he bit down on a cyanide capsule he had in his mouth and died choking on his own vomit on the floor of the barracks. This was a fitting end for the chicken farmer who would cleanse humanity by raising a race of true Aryans.

Two years after the war was over Georg returned home to Munich. What he returned to was certainly not what he left. Hitler had told the German people that in ten years they wouldn't recognize their country. He meant that he was going to transform it into an earthly paradise. His promise came true in that the people were no longer able to recognize their country especially in the cities. They couldn't even find the block they lived on never mind the building or house! The Allied bombing had done it's job. Everything was rubble. There were no services and people were doing the most desperate things just to get something to eat.

Although over half of his city was destroyed the people moved on and rebuilt with the help of the Marshal Plan. Georg was an accomplished artist and wrote two books about his exploits with drawings of the various cartoon logos the U-boats sported during the war. One was entitled "U-boat emblems of World War II 1939-1945". The other was "Between Greenland and Gibraltar: Experiences of a submarine radioman in peace, war and captivity"; ("Zwischen Grönland und Gibraltar: Erlebnisse eines U-Boot-Funkers in Frieden, Krieg und Gefangenschaft"). As far as I know this is only available in German. He became an art professor at a university in Munich.

Jim went on with his life just as before. After the rescue the St. Anne was frapped upside down on the slip during another one of the gales that sweep through the area. A strong gust of wind lifted the boat and smashed it to pieces on the cliff nearby. My father told me, "It made matchwood out of her". Luckily he had her insured, but she couldn't be replaced. The good little boat had done its job.

They had plans for the lifeboat which they would claim as salvage. They were hoping to disassemble it and build two boats from its timbers, but one day the Irish Navy showed up and towed it away. Ireland was under the Emergency Act and the fishermen had no recourse.

Not long after this, he was down near the shore gathering rack, a type of long broad seaweed that the farmers spread on their land for fertilizer. He had an ass and creels and a length of rope with him to tie the bundles. A friend of his was fishing nearby with a drop line from the rocks. Suddenly a freak wave came in and swept him out to sea. My father heard his cry for help, ran down to the rocks with the rope, threw it to him and pulled him to safety.

Years later when he told me about this I asked him if the man had to swim or had a hard time reaching the rope. He replied with that wistful smile of his as he looked off into the distance as if seeing it in his mind's eye and said calmly, "It went right into his hands". This man never forgot what he had done for him and whenever they met in town or near any pub, he would insist on bringing him in for a drink. That totaled seventeen men that owed their lives to my father.

After the war he married a young colleen that loved him all her life. Her name was Una Kelly. The Kelly and the McLoughlin families had been close for years. They fished together and shared the same political ideology. They were staunch Fianna Fail Republicans who wanted nothing to do with England. When my grandfathers met or would visit each other they spoke exclusively Gaelic; English was their second language. Una bore Jim two boys. My brother, Jimmy in 1947 and then I came along three years later.

We were both born in our maternal grandfather's house. There was no running water; it had to be brought in with buckets from the local well down by the cliffs near the slip. There was no electricity; the light came from oil lamps and the only heat came from the turf fires in the rooms. A midwife nurse and my grandmother brought us into the world.

When my father's father was dying he wasn't in full possession of his faculties. Taking advantage of this, a younger brother had him sign over the land to him instead of to my father whom he had promised it to. The eldest brother, John, had been living in America for years and was settled with a good job, wife and children, and had no intention on going back to Ireland. It was taken for granted that my father would inherit the land. Now he found himself basically with nothing except a wife and two small children to provide for. He had no land and although willing and able to do anything for work there was little to be found. He worked building and repairing roads and houses and any other job that needed doing, but there just wasn't enough work to be had. What he was able to earn by fishing wasn't enough.

My mother was very unhappy. We were living in a small thatched cottage my father had built on a piece of land a cousin of his let him stay on. She spent most of the time in Clougher just down the road at her parent's house while my father was out fishing or working. Every day she would bring us down and spend the day there doing chores around the farm and caring for my brother and I until my father came home. She felt desperate and decided to write a letter to her eldest sister, Mary, who immigrated to America quite a few years before. She also had another sister, Anne, and a brother, Mike, living there as well. She asked Mary if she would sponsor my father to immigrate to America.

Although they dearly loved Ireland, their families and friends, they realized they couldn't make a decent living for their children without any land of their own and very little work available. Economic stagnation caused many to leave Ireland during the 1950's. Anyone who would sponsor an immigrant would be taking full responsibility for that person legally, medically and financially. The alien seeking entry had to go through a thorough background check and be in good health. My aunt Mary knew my father well and knew that she would never regret bringing him to the United States.

The ship landed in New York and some of the family was there to greet him and bring him up to the Bronx where they all lived. My father rented an apartment in the same building as my mother's brother, Mike, in the South Bronx on 138th St. between Willis Ave and Brook. It was Mike's old apartment on the 4th floor facing the back. He moved down a floor with his wife and two boys to an apartment facing to the front.

My father's brother John and two sisters Molly and Anne lived nearby as well. All were within walking distance except my aunt Mary who owned a private house in the north Bronx in the Kingsbridge section. She was married to a good hard working Kerry man who had a job with the railroad.

The plan was for my father to set everything up and he would bring us over the following year. He got a job making coffins. It certainly wasn't to his liking, but at least he got to work with wood. He worked hard at anything he could get on the side and just about always had two jobs. He worked Saturdays as well, but never on Sunday. Little by little he bought or was given furniture by relatives to set up a proper home for us.

At night he would lie awake although tired from his days work and after his prayers he would stare at the dark ceiling and long for home. He missed the life he had known although much of it was toil and poverty. This land was so strange to him. He was living in a box on top of, under and surrounded by other boxes. A few scraggly trees were in the yards between the tenements on 139th St. and 138th.

When he looked out the window of any room all he saw was other windows and brick walls and clothes lines. No rolling meadows of grass and fields of crops; no gentle hills and distant mountains and for the first time in his life he awoke and went to sleep without the soothing sound of the sea as it washed in on the banks. The gentle sound was like a mother shushing her child to sleep. Most of all he missed his little family and the tears would slip from the corners of his eyes and flow down into his hair and onto the pillow. Although he had friends and relatives near him he still felt so alone.

True to form he had us over in nine months instead of a year and was there to meet us at the ship with a taxi and some of the relatives. After a party at Aunt Mary's we went to our apartment and settled in. It was all so strange to us. There was no building as big as ours in the whole town of Ballina except for the cathedral. We were poor but much better off than we were in Ireland since we had an income. Few around us were well off so we didn't notice.

Most of the family who had been in America were better established. A few of my uncles had Civil Service jobs which was the most sought after. Most of the relatives had come over when they were single and met and married their spouses in America where their children were born. Our situation was different. We were a whole family right off the boat from Ireland.

My father had a steady job as well as side jobs and he told my mother that all she had to do was take care of the kids and house and he would provide everything else. After his days work he would go with his friend Sam, to Brooklyn to build convalescent homes for the elderly. Any other construction jobs that were available he was always willing to take. He liked to work. He felt that when he worked with his hands his mind was free and creative. Every payday he would hand over his money to my mother to run the house. She would give him a small allowance for the week.

When he became eligible he went and applied for Citizenship. My father loved America and would often say, "God bless America; she gave me everything I have". The following year my mother became a Citizen as well. My brother and I became citizens automatically as children but we had to go down to Manhattan when we each turned 14 and officially renounce our allegiance to Ireland and take the oath of allegiance to the United States of America. I admit that I felt a bit torn between my love for both countries.

During those early years my father came home from work always in the dark. Sometimes my brother and I would already be in bed. My mother would be there to give him his dinner and sit and talk for a while. But Sunday was his day off and after Mass we would just take it easy or walk to Randal's Island or St. Mary's Park for the day and have a picnic.

I knew things were improving a bit when he would reach into his pocket and give us some money to go down to Maggie's candy store to buy a six pack of Coke. We would sit in the living room and savor our treat on a hot summer day. Sometimes a man playing a fiddle or an accordion or a hurdy-gurdy would show up in the back yard playing and singing and the people would throw coins out the window to them.

When we arrived I was just going on three years old and after a while I became very sick. It might have been the change in food or the environment. One day a little boy is taken by the hand by his big brother as they sneak out looking for bird's nests in the bushes and the next day he is living in an overcrowded tenement in the Bronx with cock roaches, mice, and the occasional rat. It was like moving to another planet.

Cheerios, a hardboiled egg and toast were about all I could stomach. I was catching just about every childhood disease as well as the common cold. I had tonsillitis, whooping cough, mumps, measles, chicken pox; whatever came along I got. They took me to doctors but nothing helped. The greatest fear at the time was polio, and a case of pneumonia could be deadly. I was weak and at one point my Aunt Mary said to my mother, "I'm afraid you might loose him, Una".

74

I remember lying in bed and my mother would be making dinner. Everything seemed quiet and gloomy and it always seemed to be dark outside. I could see her through our bedroom door that opened into the kitchen. My father would come home and kiss her and I could hear him ask her how I was. Then, while my mother prepared his meal, he would come in and lie down in the bed next to me and tell me stories. They would be about some heroic feat he performed that day like jumping on the subway tracks and saving some little boy, who was always just about my age, from an oncoming train. He never mentioned the Canton or the man he pulled from the sea.

Finally one of the relatives suggested a doctor who virtually saved my life. He was a crusty old Jewish doctor named Tanenbaum of all things and he had no qualms about scolding a patient whether a child or an adult. He prescribed a tonic for me and since my father was underweight as well he told him to take it too. Both of us would take a spoon of it together each day. Gradually my appetite came back and both of us began gaining weight. My health improved remarkably and by the time I started going to school I was a typical kid running around and playing sports with the rest of them.

My parents sent us to Catholic schools even though the tuition money could have been used for other needs. But a good education is what they insisted on and a bad report card meant trouble. My mother washed our shirts in the tub with a scrubbing board and had them ironed every day. She had us clean and neat and ready for school although I remember many times not being able to sit comfortably at my desk because of the stitches on the seat of my pants. Sometimes the other kids would laugh at me, but I got over it. She brought us the two blocks to St. Jerome's every day until we were old enough to go by ourselves.

Our apartment was different than the rest of the apartments in the building and I never could figure out why. There was an extra room that also had its own door out on the landing. We called it "the back room" and my father used it as a workshop. He was glad to have a place where he could work in his limited spare time. He had to keep his hand in what he had known and loved in a life that was changed forever.

I remember the parts of a violin he was building. The face, back and sides as well as the neck and scroll were skillfully made but not assembled. I was amazed at how he had chiseled a thick piece of wood to the gently bowed thin face and back with the F holes beautifully cut into the face. The side pieces were shaped with the curves and contours as well. It was never assembled but there is one he built in my cousin's house in Ireland and later after he retired he built another one that he gave to my nephew.

He also did something that was curious to me at the time. He bought a netting needle and some line and began making a fish net. Even at that young age I knew it was very unlikely he would ever use it; so why was he making it? He probably knew he would never use it as well. Later on I realized that it was his way of keeping in touch with what he loved most in his past life; fishing. To him it was like my mother knitting sweaters for us. I often think of the back room and that violin that would never sing a note and that net that would never taste the sea.

He was also a pretty good artist. He had no training but he was good at drawing and he painted two pictures on canvas. One of course was a steamer at sea and the other a picture of Our Lady of Fatima. They showed talent but need of instruction. I loved to draw as well and he gave me many pointers on anatomy and perspective. I eventually took up painting and still enjoy it.

The neighborhood was never good and you had to be tough to get along. If you couldn't make it on the streets, you stayed home with mommy. There was a big public school, PS-9 that straddled the block giving access through it to 139th St. by way of the schoolyards. There was a small schoolyard on one side and a much larger one on the other side of the school. This was our usual hangout where we played stickball, off the point, and basketball for the few that could afford one. Many kids played there and those that didn't attend Catholic school went there.

Each year after Christmas people would throw their old dried up trees out on the street to be picked up by the sanitation truck. The kids would burn them. One night a friend of ours gathered a few trees and broke into the school and set fire to them. The school burned to the ground. All that was left was some large piles of charred bricks. It eventually was leveled and I don't know if they ever rebuilt it.

We loved going up town to visit Aunt Mary since the neighborhood was nice with mostly private houses and plenty of trees. Kids need trees. My father would help my uncle Dan with repairs and projects around the house and my brother and I would hang out with our cousins. Later on we would all sit down to dinner together. There were lots of laughs and good times. We hated the ride home to the south Bronx and its tenement lined busy streets.

Gradually the neighborhood started getting worse and the teenage Irish and Italian gangs were reluctant to give up "turf" to the newly arrived Puerto Rican gangs. Inevitably gang wars erupted. Rookies from the Police Academy were called out for backup. It got so bad at one point that about a dozen or so would be marched by a police sergeant in their distinctive gray shirts in double files with two being dropped off at each corner. They had a reputation of using their night sticks to impress the regular police. Groups of five teenagers or more were not allowed to congregate. It was almost like marshal law.

Crime was rising due to heroin. My aunt Anne had her pocketbook snatched on her way home from visiting us. One day the teenager that lived upstairs came home from school and dropped dead on the floor. He was also the "war lord" for one of the local Puerto Rican gangs. Everyone expressed their sympathies to the parents and I heard his father tell my mother that his son had been sick, but everyone knew he died of a heroin overdose.

This and the violence that was going on around us was what I was exposed to by the age of ten. Raising kids in a big city is child abuse. Kids shouldn't be sitting on a stoop or playing in a totally depressed situation with sirens, honking horns and sometimes gunshots heard around them. They need fresh air and trees around them and grass beneath their feet, not pollution, bricks and concrete. We kids were interested in stick ball and skelly and the different "seasons" that would come along like tops or yoyos or the scooters we built from two by fours, wooden soda crates and old roller skates.

One night an empty whiskey bottle came crashing through our living room window as we were watching TV. The police came but there was nothing they could do and they said it was probably thrown from one of the rooftops on 139th St.

One Saturday morning I awoke to the sound of breaking and exploding glass. I looked out our bedroom window facing onto a courtyard between the buildings and there were flames licking out of the window in the apartment right next to me. The firemen came and had to get at some of it by running a hose through our apartment and spraying the fire from our kitchen window. The smell of the fire stayed for quite a while. A little while after that three pellet shots came through our living room window and we knew it was time to move.

Our relatives and most of our friends had already moved and my father began to look for a house we could afford instead of renting apartments. He needed to find a "handyman special"; something that needed fixing up. His good friend, Sam, whom he worked with, took us around to many real estate offices and houses in Canarsie in Brooklyn where he lived. We looked at many houses and wanted to live in any of them, but we just couldn't afford it.

My uncle Mike had taken a job as the superintendent of a building in the north Bronx. He had his job at the telephone company and he was paid for taking care of the building as well as living rent and utility free. This is what my father went for and he found one, although my brother and I didn't relish the idea of being the "super's sons". A super is just a janitor and janitors are not very high on the totem pole in any society, but the neighborhoods in the north Bronx were nice and clean with mostly private houses and our building was the only one on a tree shaded block.

It was like being in the country for us. The landlord was a nice man who had side jobs that my father was glad to do. My first job at ten years old was washing panel wagons and small trucks with my brother on Saturday for the landlords air conditioning and re-frigeration business. My brother and I were expected to help care for the building and so we would sweep and mop the hallways and stairs, take out the garbage as well as shovel the snow off the sidewalk and help with repairs. My father showed us how to disas-semble and clean the nozzle of the oil furnace which we did each week. My mother kept the brass banisters shinning bright and you could see yourself in the mailboxes.

The neighborhood was predominantly Italian and the people were very nice and down to earth as Italians are apt to be. We were introduced to a whole new cuisine that we were totally un-familiar with. We were a meat and potato kind of family. Now we had pizza, pasta, meatballs, sausage, lasagna and a plethora of de-licious food that we had never tasted before. We became big fans and were having Italian food as much as meat and potatoes.

While we still lived in the south Bronx my father seriously in-jured his back and spent a few days in the hospital. Later on after we had moved he hurt it again and knew that he was unable to do any heavy labor after that. Although free rent, utilities and a small salary as the superintendent and side jobs was great he still needed a job to make ends meet and put a little aside for the future.

My mother's sister Anne was married to a very nice gentleman from Tipperary named Jack. He was a bank guard in Manhattan for the Chase Manhattan Bank. He told my father about an opening as a bank guard for the Chemical Bank down on Wall Street and put in a good word for him.

My father was hired and it was Heaven sent for him. After all the years of hard labor on both sides of the ocean he finally had a nice clean job with a uniform and some prestige as well. He was proud that he was given a permit to carry his pistol to and from work. The people he worked with loved him and he loved them as well.

He would come home happy, not beat. He would be home for dinner regularly since he just had to stay until everyone was out of the bank and he would lock up. During the Summer they would sit outside in front of the building on folding chairs with some of the neighbors and just pass the time gossiping. He had the time to do any odd job or just sit and enjoy the rest of his day watching television and having a beer or a glass of whiskey.

Our situation was improving. One day my father announced that he was going to buy a car. He bought a brand new Buick Skylark as he said, "Right out from the hammer". He rented a garage for it from a nice family on the next block whose son, Michele, is still one of my best friends. Later he got a chance to move to a different branch of the bank in Mt. Vernon. It was only a fifteen to twenty minute drive from home. For the first time since he came to America he could go to work without having to take the subway. He was on top of the world as he would drive home wearing his uniform in his brand new car. He'd walk around the block from the garage stopping at the candy store for the paper. He had come a long way from a small thatched cottage in Parke.

One day when I was fifteen I came home and my mother and father sat me down. They told me that my father was planning to taking a two week trip to Ireland and he wanted me to go with him. I was surprised to say the least. I wondered why he chose me and not my brother; but Jimmy had a job and a car and a girlfriend and didn't mind me going. We couldn't all go as someone had to take care of the building and my mother and brother could handle it. I found out later that it was also an attempt at curing me of some of my wild and woolly ways as a young teenager growing up in the Bronx.

So off we went on a jet. It was quite an experience for us. We had never been on plane. In those days flying was much different than it is now. The passengers dressed in suits, dresses or neat casual clothes. It was a nice affair, with a great meal and free drinks and snacks. It was the first time I had fillet mignon. We flew on Air Lingus and as the plane circled to come in for a landing, the first thing that anyone notices right away is how green everything is. It's easy to see why it's called "The Emerald Isle" and inspired Johnny Cash to write and sing, "The Forty Shades of Green".

It was while we were on the plane that something we were talking about brought up the story of the Canton. He told me the story in a way that seemed as if it was no big deal to him. I guess that it had just become a part of his life that happened long ago and he didn't give it much thought. I never heard my mother nor anyone mention it in conversation. He never told my brother about it.

I was a bit shocked at the fact that my father was a hero. I never looked at him that way before and I recalled when as a kid my friends would be talking about what their fathers had done during the war and what branch of the service they were in and I had nothing to say since my father was just a fisherman in Ireland and Ireland wasn't even in the war!

Now I had found out that he and seven other men risked their lives to save sixteen men from certain death. He didn't charge a machine gun nest or storm ashore at Normandy or Iwo Jima but he did something that not too many men can lay claim to. Because of him seventeen men went on to live and have wives and children and then grandchildren as well. Who knows how many people have and still walk the Earth; what they have accomplished and what their children have accomplished down through the years, be it good, bad or indifferent, just because he chose to "Chance it".

Ireland is beautiful. It was strange for me feeling so far away and yet at home. The countryside with its farms, animals, rolling hills and mountains as well as the castles and thatched cottages with the smell of the turf fires were all so alien to a kid from the city and yet somehow familiar. Was it from the stories my mother had told me or was it some deep memories from my childhood? I couldn't tell. But most impressive of all as we approached Clougher was the sea. The sound of it washing in on the cliffs and shore had a soothing effect. It was easy to see why the old man loved it so much.

We were treated with kindness and a civility that I wasn't used to in the rough and tumble atmosphere of New York. Everyone I met seemed as if they had known me all their lives such was their warmth and kindness. They were people from a rural background and there was a sharp contrast with the brash and often rude behavior I was used to. They seemed more civilized.

Everyone was happy to see my father after so long. I could see that the people had a lot of respect for him. We stayed with my uncle James, my mother's brother, and his wife Kathleen and my four cousins. They lived in the same house, and my father and I slept in the same bed that I was born in. My aunt Kathleen treated me as good as her own children.

We went fishing with the men "walking" the salmon nets and hauling in the silvery catch. It was almost like stepping back in time as there was still a lack of some modern conveniences. My uncle James would play the accordian and sing at the local pub which was part of the house next door at "The Munnelli's", now known as "Bessies".

I thought it was all wonderful and I felt almost as if I belonged there more than in New York. Sometimes at night I would sit out-side amazed at all the stars that I never saw from the Bronx. In the background was the never-ending sound of the sea. The Kelly's couldn't do enough for us and the two weeks flew by. When we were leaving the tears were genuine.

My brother Jimmy married his girlfriend, a beautiful girl named Lucia who lived in our building. The wars in Indo-China were raging and rather than waiting to get drafted he joined the Air Force. When he and my father were talking about it one day I said that I would probably have to worry about the same thing a few years later. They laughed and said it would be long over by then since Johnson was about to start bombing North Vietnam.

Two years later I found myself in the Marines in a little combat base named An Hoa south of DaNang in the middle of an area we called "Arizona Territory" because of the cowboys and indians at-mosphere. A few years after my return I married the love of my life, a beautiful young girl from the neighborhood named Laurie whom I had know for several years. My parents had retired to Ire-land fulfilling a dream.

My life changed in a most profound way with the birth of my daughter, Kyla. Now I was a father and had to look out for the wel-fare of my baby girl. Although I had a good job at the Post Office, I didn't want to raise her in the Bronx. I wanted her to have trees and grass and most of all safety and the Bronx wasn't the place for any of that.

I looked into getting a transfer to some other branch in a nice town anywhere in the country, but was told I would have to make a mutual swap with someone else in the office I wanted. I knew that no one from a nice town would want to work in Mt. Vernon Distribution Center just north of the Bronx, so the quickest way I thought of to get out was to join the Marines again and see about making it a career.

I found that it was entirely different being a young 18 year old on my way to war than it was being a 27 year old in peacetime with a wife and child. It was impossible to make ends meet on the salary of a Private First Class. I got along great with the men who called me "Pops" because I was all of twenty seven. Not so well with the officers who were all younger and knew that the men looked up to me rather than them since I was a combat veteran with ribbons on my chest. I left after my enlistment, but I had no intention on going back to live in the Bronx so we took my parents up on their invitation to come to live with them in Ireland.

I got a job working for a German tool company within walking distance in the town of Ballina. I worked my way up to becoming a forger operating a forge making automotive tools. From raw billets to chrome finished product, every tool that left the factory was stamped "Made In West-Germany". Just after starting there I asked one of the fore-men about it, and he just gave a short puff of laughter and said satirically, "Sure if it said made in Ireland, who'd buy it? Paddy can't make anything!" So here were Irishmen making tools marked made in West-Germany for a Swedish tool company. This was my first encounter with multinational corporations.

The people were warm and we made many friends. Laurie gave birth to my son and my father became immediately attached to him. As far as he was concerned, the Sun rose and set on Michael. But no matter how comfortable we were it just never felt like home. We were all still "Yanks". The weather was a factor as well. It rained much more than we were used to. I often said that if the weather was better in Ireland there would be standing room only. Finally after over three years; the year after Michael was born, we decided to come home to America.

There was no way my mother and father would let us leave with their two grandchildren so they decided to put the house up for sale and come back with us. They were just looking for an excuse since even though they never lost their "Brogue", they always considered themselves Americans. We had no intention on going back to the Bronx. Jimmy had bought a house in a lovely little New England town in Connecticut and we all moved there.

Laurie and I rented a condominium and my parents rented a nice walk in apartment at the senior citizens housing development in town. We were together again and spent holidays and weekends enjoying ourselves around Jimmy's pool or fireplace. My parents sat back and watched with love and enjoyment as their grandchildren grew and played together.

In the late 1980's my brother started doing some research on the sinking of the Canton. This was before computers and I really have to hand it to him on how well he did. He contacted the Swedish shipping company that owned the Canton and also the last survivor that he could find, Thurs Malm. Thurs sent two letters thanking my father for saving his life and telling of his ordeal.

My brother had the local newspaper do an article on the rescue. A representative of the Swedish Merchant Marine working in New Jersey heard the story. He asked the Swedish government to officially honor my father for his action. After the rescue the men of the St. Anne were offered a plaque with their names engraved on it or eight pounds as a reward. Being practical as well as poor they easily opted for the money. So up to this time there was never any recognition of what these bold Irish fishermen had done.

My brother was contacted and arrangements were made for a presentation. A party was planned and everyone we knew was invited. It was held at the senior citizens center where they lived and it was packed. One of the neighbors took care of preparing a delicious assortment of food and there was plenty of beer, wine, spirits and soda.

The local newspaper that had done the story on him earlier was back again to cover the event and a picture was published of the Swedish government representative, Anders Sjodin presenting him with a silver goblet with his name and the date of the rescue engraved on it. He was also presented with a gold tie clasp with the sailing ship logo and a Swedish fisherman's knife from the shipping company, Brostroms, that owned the Canton. It was quite a day and everyone enjoyed themselves. He had finally received some recognition for what he had done.

I had to pass by where they lived on my way to and from work and made it a habit of stopping in every day just to check on them and make sure everything was alright. My father was in his eighties and his heart wasn't what it should be. He had already undergone an operation for a carotid artery and one day we got a call from my mother telling us that he had had a stroke and the ambulance was on the way. He survived it and though it took some time for him to regain his speech, with the help of a wonderful therapist, he was pretty much back to normal.

One day I dropped by and Lucia had taken my mother shopping and he was alone in the living room just looking out the window. He didn't care too much for television but always watched the news and a few other shows he liked, but when my mother wasn't home it wasn't unusual for him to just sit and ponder.

I came in and kissed him hello and asked what he was doing just to make conversation. He said, "Ah, thinking I was". "Thinking of what?" I asked. He looked at me and said, "I was just thinking of the time of the Canton", and as he turned and looked out the window I knew it was not the rolling Berkshires he was seeing nor the nicely manicured lawns and ornamental trees. He was at the tiller of the lifeboat and the sea was raging and the wind howling in his ears as the huge boat was pitching and rolling in the storm. He was soaking wet with salt spray on his lips and a sore shinbone as his crew strained at the oars to bring the big half waterlogged boat and the sixteen men ashore to safety.

Six months later he lay on his deathbed surrounded by friends and family as a close family friend led us in the Rosary. He had the Last Rites and in two weeks he would be eighty three. His doctor had arranged for us to have a private room on the top floor in an out of the way part of the hospital with a bed in it if one of us wanted to stay over night or take a nap. He was in and out of consciousness for two weeks and it was very hard on us.

One night my mother and I were there alone. My brother was exhausted and I told him to go home and I would call him and keep him posted. I lied down on the bed and fell into a light sleep and woke to the sound of voices. My mother was crying softly and asking the nurse if he was gone. The nurse replied that he was.

I jumped out of bed and she told us to speak to him in his ear as the sense of hearing is the last to go. We told him we loved him and the nurse cried along with us as if she was a relative. I said to her, "Surely you must be used to this by now", and she said to me, "You never get used to it". She left for the doctor to make the final pronouncement and we kissed him goodbye. I kissed his hands that had worked so hard to feed clothe and shelter us as well as his feet that had walked so many miles on our behalf. The priest came in and said a few words of comfort and we left the room.

We stepped off the elevator and left the hospital openly sobbing and in tears. People stared at us and must have realized the reason for our grief. How ironic it was to see people getting on the elevators with balloons for a newborn and flowers for loved ones and us feeling such a loss. Although it was a bright cold winter day I don't know how I drove home through the mist. Everything seemed different. Everything was different. Something that was always there was suddenly gone. Something was missing. We had never lived in a world without him.   The End

THE CREWS

The Crew of the Canton

The lost

G. Torssell (Captain), G. Rausis, E. Andersson, K. Johnson, I. Olsson, A. Andersson, S. Heikel, F. Lundin, O Bondesson, O. Bakken, S. Roos, K. Pattersson, S. Eklund, C. Vincent, K. Lorenz, A. Espinilla.

The survivors

Nills Westberg, Paul Wihlborg, Oscar Johannesson, Karl Torsson, Evald Andersson, Karl Johansson, Thurs Malm, Agne Kortz, Erling Andersen, Harald Kristiansen, Ove Olofsson, Nils Ekberg, Zosimo Tabudlong.

The Crew of the St. Anne

James McLoughlin (Skipper), William Knox, Michael McLoughlin (James' brother), John McLoughlin (cousin), Thomas Hughes, William Hughes, John Kelly. John Langan.

IRELAND: INIS FÁIL - THE ISLAND OF DESTINY

A brief History of an ancient land

"The great Gaels of Ireland are the men that God made mad,
For all their wars are merry, and all their songs are sad."

G.K. Chesterton the Ballad of the White Horse

I reland is a strange and mystical land. From ancient times the history of the people of that island has been wrapped in mist and legend. Evidence of human presence in Ireland goes back to 10,500 BC. The bone of a bear with clear markings of some cutting tool as well as shellfish remains and evidence of fishing have been found from this period..

Some of the oldest man made structures in the world are in

Ireland. New Grange in County Meath was built during the Neolithic period about 3,200 BC. It is older than Stonehenge and the Pyramids. Though believed to be a burial site, its use remains a mystery, and on the morning of the Winter Solstice the rising Sun sends a shaft of light down the passageway that floods the inner chamber.

Many secrets are buried below the bogs. The Céide Fields in northern Mayo are the oldest system of fields found in the world. Archeologists have found walled off fields, houses and Megalithic tombs from over six thousand years ago. Tree rings from ancient logs dug up from under the bog that developed over the years show that the climate was warmer at that time leading to almost year round cultivation. These tree rings show various cold and warming spells which have occurred throughout this final phase of our last ice age.

During the Ice Age Ireland and Britain were connected to mainland Europe. As the climate changed and the ice receded the seas rose until the island was cut off from Briton about 12,000 years ago; over 6 thousand years before Briton was cut off from the rest of Europe. This left Ireland isolated for quite some time.

Little is known of the first inhabitants of the island. There were several different peoples and their history is a mixture of truth and legend. The Tuitha Da Danan were for some time the occupants of the Island until they were replaced by a peoples called the Milesians, the Gaels, the first Celtic tribe to reach Ireland.

THE CELTS

Deep peace of running waves to you, Deep peace of the flowing air to you, Deep peace of the smiling stars to you, Deep peace of the quiet earth to you, Deep peace of the watching shepherds to you, Deep peace of the Son of peace to you.

Ancient Celtic Blessing

The Celts came to Ireland during the Iron Age. A great part of Europe was occupied by them. They ranged from what is now Switzerland and northern Italy to France and the Iberian Peninsula, as well as, Briton and Ireland. In 400 BC they sacked Rome and a century later they swept through the Balkans and conquered Greece; sacking Delphi and went on to parts of Asia minor which was Persia and eventually set up a nation called Galatia which is in modern day Turkey. The Romans called its inhabitants Galli (Gauls or Celts). St. Paul established a Church there in the first century hence his "Epistle to The Galatians".

Ireland was first mentioned in the 6th century BC in a text called The Massiliote Periplus. A Periplus is what the ancient Greeks called a type of log or sailing manual used by their navigators.

The Massiliote Periplus records a voyage of exploration from the Greek city which is now Marseille on the Mediterranean coast of France. Sailing the coast of Spain they passed through the Straits of Gibraltar and turned north exploring the coast of Portugal and on to the British Isles. They mentioned "The Blessed Isle" or Lerne, the Greek name for Ireland, which was located to the west of Albion, their name for Britain. Later, about 325 BC, Pytheas Massiliensis a Greek geographer sailed from Marseille to Albion, mentioned Lerne, went as far as Scandinavia and was the first to describe "The midnight sun".

From the classic writings of the Greco-Roman world, the people of Lerne were savage and inhospitable. Strabo, who was a very ethnocentric pro Roman Greek, said they were more hostile than the Britons and were "man-eaters" which was the usual disparagement aimed at a fearsome enemy. Pomponius Mela also wrote that the Irish were more savage than any other race. He reported that Ireland was so rich in grass that cattle would burst from eating too much if unrestrained.

The Celts were headhunters. They believed that the head held the soul and they kept the heads of their vanquished enemies as trophies. In his 1st-century History Diodorus Siculus, had this to say about Celtic head-hunting:
"They cut off the heads of enemies slain in battle and attach them to the necks of their horses. The blood-stained spoils they hand over to their attendants, striking up a paean and singing a song of victory; and they nail up these first fruits upon their houses, just as do those who lay low wild animals in certain kinds of hunting. They embalm in cedar oil the heads of the most distinguished enemies, and preserve them carefully in a chest, and display them with pride saying for this head one of their ancestors, or his father, or the man himself, refused the offer of a large sum of money. They say that some of them boast that they refused the weight of the head in gold".

He described the Celts of Gaul: *"The Gauls are tall of body with rippling muscles and white of skin and their hair is blond, and not only naturally so for they also make it their practice by artificial means to increase the distinguishing color which nature has given it. For they are always washing their hair in limewater and they pull it back from the forehead to the nape of the neck, with the result that their appearance is like that of Satyrs and Pans since the treatment of their hair makes it so heavy and coarse that it differs in no respect from the mane of horses. Some of them shave the beard but others let it grow a little; and the nobles shave their cheeks but they let the moustache grow until it covers the mouth."*

They were skillful in working gold and silver into beautiful jewelry as well as iron into weapons and tools. The torcs and bracelets as well as the brooches like the Tara Broche and other gold and silver artifacts remain as a testament to this.

They were innovators as well. They developed a reaper that would be pushed ahead of an ox or horse much like a giant hair clipper. This was over a thousand years before Cyrus McCormack invented his. They also used soap when most of the ancient world used olive oil to clean their body. They developed a way of putting an iron tire on a cart or chariot wheel in one piece instead of welding or riveting separate pieces together. After the tire was forged in one continuous circular band it would be heated to expansion and then put on the wooden wheel and when it cooled the tire was permanently fixed.

They lived by tribal laws which could vary greatly. Women, in many cases were co-equal with men in property and marital rights. Some women were warriors and even led men into battle. Cattle raiding leading to war was common. The great Irish epoch, the Táin Bó Cúailnge, or "Cattle Raid of Cooly", is based on a war between Queen Mebd of Conaught and the king of Ulster, her former husband, over a prize bull.

The Celts, like many other primitive people, went into battle virtually naked sometimes spiking their hair, using war paint and brandishing swords, spears, shields, bow and arrow. They ran or rode on horseback or in light chariots with thick wicker sides. They used these chariots well against the Romans in Gaul and Briton long after the Romans and other ancient armies had disregarded them and used them mainly for ceremonial purposes. Sometimes they went into battle with their giant wolf hounds as war dogs. These dogs were feared and valued throughout Europe.

It's been said that the greatest non-event in Irish history is the fact that the Romans never got there. Julius Caesar was the first Roman to write about the island and considered the people to be fearsome; living a miserable life in a cold inhospitable land which he named Hibernia or the "Cold Land".

The Celts had lived for hundreds of years without any outside influence. There has been archeological finds such as coins and artifacts showing there was some contact but nothing to show any permanent Roman presence. Although there were plans for an invasion it never materialized. But there was some trade between the two cultures as well as many raids by the Irish upon Roman Britannia. Roman influence was shown in the Celtic manner of dress as well as some artifacts.

The Romans called the people of Hibernia Scoti, as did the early Greeks. Their name for England was Britannia and the people were known as Britons who were Celts. The northern part of the island of Britain, now called Scotland, was called Caledonia after the Caladoni, a major Celtic tribe. Many Celtic tribes in Caledonia were called Picts because they painted their bodies before going into battle.

The Scoti began settling and associating with their Celtic cousins the Caladoni as well as with the Welch and Celts of Cornwall. Toward the end of the Roman occupation of Britannia various groups of Germanic tribes especially the Jutes, Angles and Saxons began raiding Britain on a large scale. They never reached Ireland.

Around 500 AD a Gaelic kingdom known as Dál Riata was established by Erc a king in the north of Ireland. It encompassed Ulster province and the kingdom of Argyle in Caledonia. Soon so many Scoti crossed the Irish Sea and were living in this northern part of Britain that it no longer was known as Caledonia but Scotland.

The rulers of Scotland all traced their descent to Fergus Mòr Mac Earca the son of Erc. Fergus brought with him what is known as "The Stone of Destiny" or "The Stone of Scone" (pronounced "Skoon"). Legend has it that it was Jacobs's pillow on which he slept and dreamt of Angels ascending and descending a ladder. It was used since ancient times as the Coronation Stone upon which sat the Ard Ri or High King of Ireland.

When brought over by Fergus it was kept at the monastery at Scone, in Scotland, and on this stone the kings of Scotland were coronated until it was stolen by Edward I of England in 1296 as "spoils of war". Now the Stone of Scone is placed beneath the Royal Throne at Westminster Abby where all English monarchs are crowned up to and including Queen Elizabeth II in 1952. One wonders why they leave so much value on this stone.

After the fall of the Roman Empire, Europe descended into the "Dark Ages". At the very edge of this darkness was a small light that would illuminate minds as well as manuscripts. Western classic learning both Latin and Greek flourished in a relatively secluded Hibernia due to the one greatest thing that did reach Ireland from the Romanized world which was to become the cornerstone of Irish culture, art and life.

THE ISLE OF SAINTS
AND SCHOLARS

I rise today
Through a mighty strength,
the invocation of the Trinity,
Through belief in Threeness
Through confession of Oneness
of the Creator of creation.

From St. Patrick's Breastplate

Christianity came to Ireland probably through missionaries from Britain and Brittany since they had accepted Christianity after the Romans made it the state religion. There were Christians in Ireland before the arrival of St. Patrick. In 430 AD, Paladius, a British Bishop was sent to Ireland by Pope Celestine to minister to "Scots believing in Christ", which indicates that Christianity was there before Patrick arrived. At any rate, St. Patrick was not the first to bring Christianity, but he was the most successful.

After being kidnapped from Roman Britannia by Irish pirates he was sold into slavery. He was taken to the west of Ireland, many believe to a place now called Fohill in Mayo, where he tended sheep. After several years of cruel and harsh treatment he escaped and made his way home. In a dream he heard the Irish calling him back to bring them the Word of God. After being ordained a priest and becoming a bishop St. Patrick came back to where he had been held as a slave and founded a Church at Killala near Fohill as well as many others.

On his way to what is now known as "Crough Patrick", which was a mountain held sacred by the Druids, he found that a local Christian named Cummins had already begun converting the pagans in an area beyond Fohill. This peninsular headland, where I was born, became known as Kilcummin or Cummins Church. Christianity in Kilcummin predated St. Patrick.

Converting these savage heathens was quite a task for the missionaries especially since they had to contend with the powerful pagan priestly class; the Druids. They were not only shamans but also judges, lawyers, advisors, poets and scholars teaching by tradition the ancient ways of the Celts. They held power over the chieftains and kings of the island.

Eventually the new faith took hold and paganism was suppressed. But just as in the rest of Europe people still clung to some of the old ways and sometimes incorporated them into the new faith. Monasteries which were like small villages arose throughout the island. The populations could be quite numerous considering all the functions that needed to be done for the community to survive let alone thrive. They were an oasis of education and culture.

Some of the monks spent endless hours copying rare classic books and especially the beautiful and intricately illuminated copies of the Bible. Using gold, silver and jewels, skilled craftsmen adorned Manuscripts like the Book of Kells and Sacramentals used at Mass and Church services. The Challis of Armagh, the Derrynaflan Patan and the Cross of Cong attest to the beautiful work that these forgotten craftsmen wrought.

From these monasteries went forth missionaries to Britain and the rest of Western Europe to teach and keep the Faith alive. With the fall of the Empire civilization took a turn and what followed was mostly chaos. Since the Empire never reached Ireland, its fall had no effect. With the breakdown of authority and the decay of roads and trade routes in continental Europe, Germanic tribes ran about plundering and occupying land at will. The Angles, Saxons and Jutes virtually took over what was Roman Britain. The Celts no longer held sway in Britain but still held Scotland, Wales and Cornwall.

A large part of continental Europe was taken over by Franks and Goths. Most of the Celts on the continent had been conquered and virtually wiped out or assimilated by the Romans long before. Ireland remained separate from all this. The Celtic Gaels were still the dominant people of the island with their own culture, laws, chieftains, kings and Church. Though fully accepting the authority of the Pope and the doctrines of the Church they had their own particular traditions and customs.

Many of the monks sailed out to evangelize the islands around Ireland, Scotland and England as well as mainland Europe. Their boats, called currachs, were built of wooden frames covered with hides stitched together and sealed with animal fat to keep them waterproof. They were powered by oars and one or two square rigged sails and had keels to withstand heavy seas and tack into the wind.

The monks traveled from Ireland throughout Europe establishing monasteries in the British Isles, France, Germany, Switzerland and Italy. They founded schools which did much to bring the Classic literature of Greece and Rome back to Continental Europe where it had been all but lost in the generations after the fall of the Empire. The Hiberno-Scottish Missions were acclaimed throughout Europe as centers of education and culture. They had a civilizing affect during a time of almost incessant warfare. Much of it was due to the conversion of the Germanic tribes to Christianity.

Ireland became known as the "Isle of Saints and Scholars". It became famous as a seat of learning throughout Europe. St. Columba founded a monastery on the island of Iona, one of the Hebrides Islands off the western Scottish coast. Its fame as a bastion of learning was well known throughout Europe. In parts of England Christianity was in decline and the paganism of the Germanic Saxons was spreading among the people. Irish monasteries sent missionaries like St. Aidan to North Umbria to bring back the faith by invitation of the new king who had been educated at Iona. Kings, nobles and those wealthy enough, sent their sons to Ireland or one of the Irish missions, (Schottenklöster; German for "Scottish monasteries"), to be educated.

This is not to say that Ireland was some bucolic paradise at the time. Kings and chieftains still waged war on each other and some were always struggling to gain the title of Ard Ri or High King of Ireland. Sometimes even the monks of different monasteries waged war on each other. But just as in all times and in all places there were times of peace. Ireland remained Celtic; removed from the rest of Europe by sea and culture.

In the early 6th century one of these seagoing monks named Brendan made many voyages around Ireland as well as sailing to Scotland, Wales, Britain and Brittany. He showed great zeal for spreading the Gospel since his ordination at the age of 28. Although there had been legends for centuries about a great island far to the west, he heard first hand about the "Blessed Isle" from one of his disciples, Barinthus, who told him he had just returned from "Paradise".

Sometime between 512 and 530 Brendan set off with 14 other monks on a voyage that would be read and talked about throughout Europe for centuries afterward and would influence and aid Columbus in his voyage to the New World. Brendan and his companions set out from the coast of Kerry after 40 days of fasting and prayer. He returned home after 7 years which in itself gives an example of the seamanship these monks possessed. It's believed by many that Brendan reached America.

In 1976 a celebrated adventurer and writer named Tim Severin proved the possibility of such a voyage by building a currach according to the description in the story using only tools and material that would be available at that time. He built it using Irish ash and oak framing lashed together with almost two miles of leather thongs. They wrapped it with traditionally tanned ox hides and then sealed it all with wool grease. It was 36 ft long and had two masts with square rigged sails on which Severin had red Celtic Crosses emblazoned. He named it the Brendan and after being blessed by the local priest and Christened by his young daughter with a bottle of Irish whiskey, they set off on their adventure.

From May of 1976 to June of 1977 they sailed over 4,500 miles from Ireland to The Hebrides, Iceland and Greenland then Newfoundland. They passed sites that could easily relate to those described by St. Brendan when looked at through the eyes of a 6th century navigator like; "Paradise of birds" and "Islands of sheep"; being the Faro Islands. Or "pillars of crystals"; being ice bergs, and "mountains that hurled rocks at voyagers"; like volcanoes on Iceland, and then "The Promised Land" which was probably Newfoundland. The boat is now in the Craggaunowen museum in County Clare.

From New Hampshire to Massachusetts to Connecticut and as far as West Virginia and other states, archeological sites have been found that many believe to be Celtic. Markings on stones found in West Virginia have been interpreted as Ogham, a type of writing used by the Celts in the early middle ages. Of course this is denied by most scholars, but for years they believed that the Viking Sagas about reaching America were just legends. Then in 1961 a Viking settlement was found in L'Anse aux Meadows near the northern tip of Newfoundland.

Usually wherever these Irish monks went they would build small monastic cells shaped like beehives where they could live and pray. These beehive structures are found throughout Ireland and excellent examples can be seen on Skellig Michael, a spectacular island off the coast of Kerry where they built a monastery. Stone Irish beehive structures as well as their way of marking the Winter Solstice with shafts of light as in New Grange have been found in New England and there is a particularly mysterious site at a place called "Gungiswap" in Groton Connecticut.

These structures could not have been built by American Indians. There is no evidence of anything like them in all of pre-Columbian North America. Viking Sagas recorded that wherever they went on their voyages west, they found traces of "The Westmen" that had been there before them. These were Irish monks fleeing the "Northmen".

The Vikings called themselves Ostmen or Austmenn – "East-men". The Irish they referred to as "Vestmenn" or Westmen. Irish monks had a settlement on Iceland although there were no people there! Many of them sought only seclusion and prayer like the reclusive desert Saints of Egypt and the Middle East. Their only desert was the sea and they would "exile themselves for Christ" by putting out to sea in a currach and trusting in God to bring them where He wanted them to go or swallow them up in the depths. But they were ever exploring westward in search of the Blessed Isle.

THE VIKINGS

"From the fury of the Northmen,
Oh Lord deliver us"

Prayer of the Celtic monks

L ike a slow roll of thunder from the north, starting with the first raids around 790 AD, came something that Ireland as well as the rest of Europe never expected: the Vikings.

Due to climate changes brought about by volcanic activity that spewed ash into the atmosphere, and meteor strikes churning up dust carried by the prevailing winds across the far northern parts of Europe, the people suffered from extremely cold winters during the 8th century bringing about struggles for arable land. Their farms couldn't support the population. Wars over land were frequent.

Many of the Scandinavians took to the sea with hopes of finding new lands and treasure. They would go on pirate raids. They would say they went "a Viking", sometimes bringing back the booty to Scandinavia and sometimes staying where they conquered, settled and ruled. The Norwegians and Danes went west and south. The Swedes went east and south.

With their beautifully designed and skillfully built ships they had quite an advantage over their prey. Built from thin split oak planks, using a technique called "riving", unlike the sawed timber that most other peoples used, their "Drakon Ships" were light, flexible, and strong. They could sail in heavy seas or along a coast line and with the ship's shallow draft they could sail up rivers and raid villages, towns and monasteries without warning. In the year 845, under the Viking Ragnar, they sailed up the Sein with 150 ships carrying thousands of warriors. They sacked and pillaged Paris untill they withdrew after being paid 2,570 kilos of silver and gold by the king.

They used various types of ships. Some were small for coastal use, some were for cargo and others were large for ocean going with up to 100 men on the oars. Perfectly proportioned by length and beam they could take on heavy seas. With a large square rigged movable sail they could tack into the wind and glide along using keel and canvas. They had such regard for these ships that they were part of their religion. Some chieftains were totally buried in them with their prized weapons and valuables as well as their dog slain at their feet. Some were placed in their ship pushed out to sea and set ablaze.

When the Vikings began raiding Ireland they were almost exclusively from Norway although later in the second wave the Danes came as well. They found that Ireland was unusual and much different than Britain and continental Europe in that there were no towns. Because of its isolation Ireland never established townships like the rest of Europe.

After the coming of the Gaelic Celts, Ireland had no outside conquest and little contact with any other civilizations for over 800 years. They were an agrarian and seafaring society with their main settlements around the strongholds of their kings and chieftains and the monasteries that had been built since their conversion to Christianity. The Vikings established trading posts at the mouths of the rivers. Dublin, Cork, Limerick, Wexford, Galway and others grew into the towns and eventually the cities that we know today. They were all originally Viking trading posts.

At this time the Irish had no coinage. Barter was the means of exchange based on the value of a cow. The Norsemen brought the concept of silver and gold coinage which was much more convenient than barter. So in a way these marauders by establishing towns and a stable economy actually brought a kind of civilization of a sort to Ireland.

At first they seldom ventured far inland preferring to stay near the coast with their ships and lines of communication back to Scandinavia. The Vikings preferred raids upon unexpecting unarmed victims rather than to take on well trained armed warriors. This is not to say that they were in any way reluctant to do battle to the death if need be with their concept of a warriors reward in Valhalla.

Another thing about the Irish that they found different than most of their other adversaries was that these Gaels were just as fierce as they were!. Vikings made their living by raiding and plundering. Many of the Irish were no different. They raided each other, the coast of Britain from Scotland to Wales and Cornwall as well as beyond to the shores of Brittany in northern France.

In the first 25 years of Viking attacks starting in 795, the annals show that there were 26 incidence of plundering by Vikings and in the same period there were 87 raids done by Irishmen upon each other! One Viking raid a year wouldn't cause any great damage, especially since attacks on monasteries and churches were common even before the Vikings came. Churches and Monasteries were always a rich source of plunder.

After the Norsemen's initial success in establishing themselves along the coast they settled into life in Ireland. They intermarried with the Gaels and became known as Hiberno-Norse or Norse-Gaels. They began speaking Gaelic and most of them converted to Christianity. They became "as Irish as the Irish themselves". They still held ties with Scandinavia and the "foreign" Vikings as well.

Eventually all Vikings in Ireland came to be known as Danes even though most had come from Norway or had been born in Ireland. Recent D.N.A. evidence from skeletal findings of Viking settlements in Greenland shows that they were more Celtic than Norse with the connections through the females. One of the main reasons for adventurous young men leaving Scandinavia was in search of wives, and the Gaelic colleens were renowned for their beauty.

As the Vikings settled into their towns, the Irish Kings and Chieftains began hitting back with a will. They raided their settlements or would fall on their expeditions sometimes slaughtering all of them and dividing the booty including their ships which they used and copied. A situation came about where there were Celtic-Gaels, Norse-Gaels, and Scandinavian Norsemen all living on the island competing with each other for land and power. Sometimes they would be allied with and against each other as the opportunity arose.

This all came to a head when Brian Baru became the High King of Ireland. He had battled the Vikings from his youth. Through typical rivalry the king of Leinster revolted and turned to the Hiberno-Viking kingdom of Dublin for help. The two sides allied against Brian and were defeated in 999. Brian accepted hostages, from the Dublin Vikings and the King of Leinster as was the custom.

As a peace gesture he gave one of his daughters, Sláine, as wife to Sitric Silkbeard Olafsson the king of Dublin. He then accepted Sitric's mother as his wife-concubine. Such practices were condemned by the Church, but the custom went on nevertheless.

Her name was Gormlaith. She was reputed to be the most beautiful woman in Ireland, but also the most devious. She is thought by many to be the main instigator for the battle that was to come. In the Njal's Saga from 13th century Iceland she is portrayed as bent on revenge on Brian Boru stating, "She was a very beautiful woman, but her best qualities were those over which she had no control, and it was commonly said that her character was evil insofar as she had control over it."

She was the daughter of M'ael M'orda Murchada, King of Leinster who had rebelled against Brian and been defeated. She was married earlier at the age of fifteen to Olaf Cuaran, the Gaelic-Viking king of Dublin and York until his death in 981. She bore him a son, Sitrig who was called Silkbeard. Her brother, Máel Mórda, had become king of Leinster after their father's death. Dublin at the time was a powerful kingdom controlling many of the islands around Ireland and Britain as well as York in England. It was the largest Viking base outside of Scandinavia.

Gormlaith hated Brian and was constantly scheming against him and insulting her brother, for submitting to him. A situation arose while Máel Mórda was visiting the court of Brian. Brian's son Murchad was involved in a chess game and Gormlaith's brother suggested a move which lost him the game. Insults flew between Murchad and Máel Mórda which resulted in the king of Leinster leaving in a rage and going home to stir up the Leinstermen once more against Brian.

Brian divorced Gormlaith and she went to her son Sitric in Dublin, and urged him to make war on the Irish. Leinster again revolted and as in the last war joined forces with the Vikings of Dublin.

Gormlaith urged her son to call on Sigurd the powerful Gaelic-Viking lord of Orkney, for help. She told him to promise anything to get the Vikings alliance. Emissaries were sent and Sitrig promised Sigurd the crown of High King of Ireland and his mother's hand in marriage. He then sent emissaries to the two Vikings lords of the Isle of Man who were brothers, Bróðir and Óspak, and promised Bróðir the same thing in reward for his help with the stipulation that he not tell Sigurd of Orkney about the arrangement.

Óspak, his brother, refused to draw his sword against Brian believing him to be a "good king" and instead threw in his lot with the Ard Ri and sailed with his men to Ireland. Sigurt of Orkney told Sitrig that he would be arriving during Holy Week. The word went out far and wide of what was about to happen. Foreign Vikings from England, Scotland, and Normandy as well as from as far away as Iceland all converged on Dublin for what would be the final battle for control of Ireland. Either the Gaels or the Vikings would be the dominant power.

The ships began arriving on Palm Sunday, sailing into the Liffy estuary. The Vikings and Leinstermen numbered over seven thousand. The Irish had an advantage in numbers especially with their Viking allies which brought their numbers to about eight thousand. Just before the battle one of Brian's allies, Malachy the king of Meath betrayed him and withdrew his three thousand men leaving Brian forces greatly diminished.

For both sides, this was it. There was no going back. Brian was in his seventies at the time. He was not the man that defeated his enemies fifteen years before. After riding through his army with them cheering; his banner flying, holding high a Crucifix, he chose to let his son and his captains do battle while he prayed and repeated the Psalms quietly in his tent as the battle began on Good Friday 23rd of April 1014.

As the Vikings sailed in they were surprised and somewhat taken aback at what they saw before them. Many had been to Ireland before usually finding a docile situation on raids with easy pickings. But now they saw a backdrop of smoke and fire from the surrounding towns and villages in league with Dublin sacked and pillaged by Brian's army. It was not what they expected.

The Vikings landed at high tide in the morning and began coming from the east as the Leinstermen and Dublin Vikings came up from the south. The carnage began at dawn and literally lasted all day until dusk. It was described in the annals by witnesses as a terribly loud and bloody battle. Most of the Vikings wore chain mail and as usual were heavily armed with battle axes, broadswords and conical helmets with nose pieces. Contrary to popular belief the Vikings nor did any other warriors have horns on their helmets. This is a theatrical prop from Germanic operas and is totally impractical for close fighting to say nothing of the use of a bow.

The Irish wore thick linen, quilted body protection and a variety of light armor from chain mail to helmets. they viewed heavy armor as unmanly. They used the usual medieval weapons especially the light javelin which they hurled against the enemy and brought many of the Norsemen down.

Brian's son, Murchad, fell fighting, his arm paralyzed from swinging his broad sword all day, but still managed to kill his adversary with a dagger as the Viking slew him. It seemed as though the battle was lost at that point when Murchad's banner fell. Sigurt of Orkney died with the "Raven Banner" that his Gaelic mother had woven for him tucked in his breast. His desire for the crown of High King of Ireland as well as the hand of Gormlaith died with him at Clontarf. The battle went on until both sides were all but exhausted.

Finally the Norse lines broke. The Vikings were driven back toward the Liffy and then it turned into a rout with them running headlong for their ships. But the ships were not there. The same high tide which had brought them in came back in the evening and the ships were scattered about the estuary. They hadn't planned on needing them to escape.

This is when it became a slaughter. The Irish drove them into the water where they were killed and drowned weighed down by their heavy chain mail. The bank of the river ran red. Brian's fifteen year old grandson, Tadc, died in the fray being smashed against one of the fishing weirs by the tide as he held onto the hair of one of the Norseman who drowned with him. Most of the Viking and Irish leaders were killed. Óspak the Viking from the Isle of Mann who allied with Brian survived but his son was killed.

His brother Bróðir and his men were in full retreat hoping to make it to Dublin when he came upon Brian's pavilion and rushed in looking for the king. He bypassed Brian taking him for an old priest. One of his men who had known the king pointed him out and Bróðir brought his battle axe down upon him ending the reign of Brian Baru. Bróðir was captured and his fate was too cruel to relate.

The battlefield was strewn with the dead of over seven thousand as well as a great number of wounded. These were the days before Chivalry was known; no quarter was given and none expected. The battle was not one of tactics or maneuver. It was man to man, champion to champion, toe to toe, shield to shield. Those who survived such battles, like the peasant soldier that couldn't escape, would be sold as a slave. A noble would be held for ransom. The wounded would rather die fighting than face a life of misery and probable starvation if they had no one to care for them.

Sitrig Silkbeard and his mother Gormlaith as well as his wife Sláine, the daughter of Brian, watched from his tower in Dublin where he had reinforcements that were of no use, as the Leinstermen and Norse were utterly defeated. Sláine, with her Irish pride taunted Sitrig and said, "It appears to me that the foreigners have gotten their inheritance...I wonder is it heat that is upon them. But they tarry not to be milked if that is it". Sitrig backhanded her in the mouth knocking out one of her teeth.

So the battle ended with most of the leaders on both sides being killed and although Sitrig and the Dublin Hiberno-Norse still continued on for a while, their power was greatly diminished.

The power of the foreign Vikings in Ireland was broken and Dublin eventually lost York to the Saxons. Other towns such as Cork, Wexford, Waterford, and Limerick still were basically "Gaelic Viking" but grew more Irish in culture and traditions. There were still raids by Vikings and Gaelic marauders but the Irish held the upper hand and ruled themselves without any outside influence. Various kings and chieftains ruled their lands with a somewhat loose allegiance to the Ard Ri. It was the end of the Viking Age as far as Ireland was concerned and once again the island was ruled by Irish kings.

THE NORMAN / ENGLISH

Oh the strangers came and tried to teach us their ways,
And scorned us just for being what we are,
But they might as well go chasing after moonbeams,
Or light a penny candle from a star.

Galway Bay

T he kings and chieftains of Ireland still waged war on each other and in one of those wars the kings united and deposed Dermot of Leinster for his excessive cruelty to his nobles as well as abducting Derbforgaill, the wife of Tiernan O'Rourke the King of Breifne, in 1152. He fled to England and asked Henry II the Norman king to help him regain his throne. Henry obliged with the backing of a Papal Bull issued by Pope Adrian IV to bring the Celtic Church into line with the Roman Rite. Before becoming Pope Adrian IV, his name was Nicholas Breakspear. He is the only Englishman that has ever been Pope.

The Celtic Church was in full accordance with Rome and they accepted the Pope's authority, but there were differences in traditions and minor observances such as the style of tonsure the monks wore. But the biggest differences was the way the two Rites calculated Easter which is too complicated to go into, and the matter of the Sacrament of Penance or Reconciliation.

On the continent they used a method of what was called Canonical Penance. For serious sins one could only get absolution from a Bishop. Penances were many times public and often very harsh. Sometimes the Penance would be suspended because of its severity.

In the Celtic Church they used what came to be called "Tariff Penance" meaning that certain penances were given for particular sins. A person could go to their local priest in private and receive absolution and it could be repeated in cases when they fell into that particular sin again. A form of this eventually became the Sacrament of Reconciliation that is used throughout the Roman Catholic Church. Penance is a private affair between the penitent, the priest and God.

The Roman Rite also disapproved of the act of going into "Exile for Christ"; monks casting themselves adrift in currachs. There was also the important matter of Tithes that Rome wanted from the Celtic Church. The rest of Europe was in line with the Roman Rite although they too had their own traditions. But the Irish Church was just too independent and what better excuse for the Norman English to conquer more territory than to do it with the blessing of the Pope and consider it a Crusade.

On May 1st, 1169, Norman mercenaries landed in Ireland with the permission of Henry and the pledge of fealty from Dermot. After seizing Lienster they began attacking other Irish kingdoms. Richard de Clare, 2nd Earl of Pembroke, known as Strongbow, one of Henry's knights, landed the following year at Bannow Strand in County Wexford with six hundred knights as well as men at arms. Dermot's promise of his beautiful warrior daughter, Aoife, as wife, and the succession of the kingdom of Leinster to Strongbow was enough to tempt any bold Norman knight. Thus began "800 years of Irish tears".

At first the Irish made a good fight of it, but eventually Henry himself came over with more warriors fearing that the Norman knights may become too independent. The Irish finally had to submit and accept Henry as the "Lord of Ireland". This, as far as the Irish were concerned, was a submission to the Pope's authority since Adrean IV claimed it as a Papal fief and appointed Henry as "Lord of Ireland'". The Celtic Church fell into line with the rest of Western Europe and accepted the Roman Rite. The Irish kings and chieftains accepted Henry as "Lord of Ireland" not "King".

As time went by, just as had happened to their distant cousins the Vikings, the Normans settled into life in Ireland. They intermarried and they and their children began taking on the culture of the Irish. They began speaking Gaelic instead of French. The Normans spoke a dialect of French that was the excepted language at the English court for several hundred years. Even after the English language was developed those from Britain who came to Ireland began speaking Gaelic.

Many of the Normans no longer considered themselves English Normans but Irish Normans. England didn't exert much control over the island directly. They were traditionally more involved with their titles, holdings and wars in France. The English monarchs satisfied themselves with the promise of fealty from the Irish and Norman nobility and kept mostly to the east coast facing Britain. After a while they controlled just the area around Dublin which was called "The Pale". Irish chieftains, kings and Irish Normans controlled the rest of the island. There was no guarantee of what might become of an Englishman who went "Beyond the Pale".

With the ascent of the Tudors to the English throne came a policy that would make the most dramatic changes ever seen in Ireland. Although there was almost constant rebellions, the Tudors unleashed the Four Horsemen that would ride the length and breath of Ireland for four hundred years. They sowed hatred that still exists to this day.

Irishmen and Englishmen had been killing each other for centuries over land and political power, but Henry VIII proclaimed himself King of Ireland and head of the Church in England and Ireland thus breaking entirely with the Pope and the Roman Catholic Church.

This is one of the most hypocritical and ridiculous situations that has ever occurred in history. Henry sought Papal permission to marry his sister in law after his brother died. The sister in law was Catherine of Aragon, daughter of King Ferdinand and Queen Isabella of Spain. She was betrothed to Arthur the heir to the English throne at the age of three in order to bring about an alliance between the Spanish empire and England in opposition to France.

They were married in their teens and Arthur died six months after the wedding. This left Henry next in line and the Pope granted him a dispensation to marry Catherine. Upon the death of his father Henry VII he became King Henry VIII and Catherine became the Queen. The people loved Catherine for her charitable work with the poor and her influencing Henry to be lenient with those involved in the "Evil May Day" riots that had taken place in London over foreigners living and working there.

The marriage produced a daughter, Mary. Catherine had several still born daughters and a son who died after seven months. Henry wanted a male heir to the throne and looked to divorce Catherine and marry Ann Bolin whom he had become enamored with. He appealed to the Pope for an annulment claiming that he felt he had committed adultery and was being cursed by God with no male offspring. The Pope refused and Henry broke with The Church.

With Anne Bolin as a sympathizer of Lutheranism and the "Reformers", her influence led Henry to take England out of the

Holy See and declare himself head of the "Church of England" thus in effect taking the place of the Pope. He declared himself "King of Ireland" as well. He then went about confiscating Church property throughout his kingdoms and persecuting anyone who didn't accept him as head of his new "Church".

The ironic part is that less than ten years before all this on 11 October 1521 Henry VIII was given the title "Defender of the Faith" by Pope Leo X. This was for a book that Henry had written, (with the assistance of St. Thomas More whom he later had beheaded), titled "Defense of the Seven Sacraments".

It was written in opposition to Luther and Protestantism, in which he defended of all things the sacrament of marriage and the supremacy of the Pope. The title was rescinded after his break with the Church and his ultimate Excommunication, but he and the following line of British monarch's right up to and including Elizabeth II still keep "Defender of the Faith" as one of their many accolades. These people are very fond of titles even when they no longer apply.

Ann Bolin gave him a daughter, Elizabeth, who would become the powerful "Virgin Queen" and was more of a king than he ever was. He eventually had Ann Bolin beheaded for "treason" as well as his next wife, Catherine Howard. Their treason was the fact that they had taken other lovers. Henry of course did whatever he wanted and had many mistresses and several illegitimate children, as well as a son, Henry Fitzroy, whom he recognized. Though few Englishmen would probably label him an "Evil King" I find it hard to call him otherwise if one is to be judged by their actions. He died a terrible death and the details of his "funeral" I will spare the reader as well as myself from thinking about.

After dubbing himself "King of Ireland" his reign turned the rebellions into religious wars. The Irish no longer fought for just material goods or political power, but for their very faith. There was no way they would except a mad English king who had become a heretic as well as a ruthless murderer that eliminated any opposition by a charge of treason and an encounter with the headsman's axe. They believed that opposing the English may cost them their life, but cooperating with them may cost them their soul. During the reign of the Tudors they passed laws that all the English in Ireland were forbidden to speak Gaelic.

The "Church of Ireland" was established with the English monarch as its head. All were required to be members and those that weren't, whether Catholic or Protestant, were persecuted and had to pay for the support of the new church anyway. This drove the Normans in Ireland, who were Catholic, even further toward the side of the Gaelic Irish. They joined forces and rebelled and this brought on a series of wars resulting in massive death from battle, famine and pestilence.

Each generation took up the cause and the retributions became more and more harsh. Finally a settlement was reached to end the fighting with the Treaty of Limerick in 1691, but it required the exile of the Irish Earls. This became known as the "Flight of the Wild Geese". Many went to France and Spain and established themselves as soldiers and statesmen. Now the English didn't have to deal with nobles organizing armies against them. But leaders inevitably rose to the cause leading armies of peasants in most cases, and would continue to do so as long as it took to be free.

During the reign of Elizabeth I they began replacing the Irish in Ulster, which was the most troublesome province, with Protestant Dissenters mostly from Lowland Scotland and Northern England. This was a double benefit for the English by getting rid of some of the Scottish dissenters and replacing the Irish Catholics with them. Most were Presbyterians; followers of John Knox and Calvinism. In this historic turnaround, the Scots were returning to where they originally had come from only now they were the pawns of the English against the Irish and the biggest difference was their religion in that they had accepted Protestantism.

The English passed a series of "Penal Laws" to further deepen the sorrows of the Irish with hopes of them dying off or immigrating to other lands. According to Edmund Burke, The Penal Laws were, "a machine of wise and elaborate contrivance, as well fitted for the oppression, impoverishment and degradation of a people, and the debasement in them of human nature itself, as ever preceded from the perverted ingenuity of man."

Catholics could not hold office or own land. They couldn't enter into a profession nor seek higher education. They were not allowed to live within 5 miles of an incorporated town. Seminaries were closed. It was against the law to celebrate Mass. The people had Mass said along hedgerows for fear of the authorities and the price on the head of a priest was the same as that on a wolf. The more the people were persecuted for their faith the stronger it became. Today there are no wolves in Ireland but there are many priests.

Times were brutal. People were thrown out of their cottages and left along the road while their land was given to foreigners. Sometimes the hovels were burned or demolished. Every rising was put down with excessive cruelty but still every generation would take up the cause for freedom. Anyone taking up arms against the crown and found guilty of High Treason was "Hanged, Drawn and Quartered"; a particularly hideous means of execution that could have only been devised in a most sadistic and diabolical mind. Yet it was the sentence meted out; as horrible as crucifixion and meant to be just as terrorizing for anyone who would even think of rebelling against the crown.

But just as crucifixion didn't stop the children of Israel from rebelling against their oppressors neither did torture, executions nor exile keep the children of Ireland from rebelling against theirs. Eventually only the leaders of rebellions would be subjugated to this sentence and they would settle for simply hanging rebels or "Transporting" them to the colonies as slave labor.

Catholic Ireland was constantly looking to Spain and France for help against their English oppressors. Spain and France were involved in intrigue and war with England long before Henry VIII broke with The Church. The English had always held claim to French territory since the time of William the Conqueror and their "privateer/pirates" were raiding Spanish vessels and territory shortly after Columbus had claimed the New World for Spain and the gold and silver came pouring into the Spanish coffers.

Several times the Spanish and French sent troops and helped in the uprisings but it was never enough to overcome the power of the English in an island so close. Each time the French or Spanish troops would be repatriated to their home and the Irish would be slaughtered, hanged, or sent to the colonies particularly Barbados to work in the cane fields. The wreck of The Spanish Armada off the west coast of Ireland dealt the Spanish a terrible blow as well as that of Irish hopes. The Armada was intended to put an end to English piracy and to hopefully conquer England.

In the seventeenth century the situation in England was confusing. Civil war had broken out. A group called Puritans who were Calvinist fanatics took up arms against the king for being too sympathetic to Catholics. The Church of England still held on to Catholic traditions and Sacraments as well as the decorative sacramentals used in church services. The Puritans felt that any acceptance of Catholicism was betraying the true spirit of "The Reformation" and wanted to purge the land of what they considered idolatry.

Their first attempt to overthrow the king failed and then one of their most ardent leaders, Oliver Cromwell, began training what he called "The New Army". They defeated the Royalists and beheaded the king. They declared parliament as the rightful authority with of course a majority of Puritans since to be otherwise was not conducive to ones health. Cromwell took the title of

"Lord Protector of the Commonwealth of England, Scotland, and Ireland". He was in effect a dictator.

Ireland was in turmoil with most of the Irish Catholics siding with the Cavaliers or Royalists and the King. Now the Irish were about to be persecuted for remaining loyal to the English king. Propaganda began to flood England about terrible atrocities committed on Protestants by the Catholics of Ireland. There were in fact atrocities on both sides but nothing to the degree that the Irish were accused of which even included cannibalism! After taking over England, Oliver Cromwell came to Ireland and they said, "He passed through like lightning".

When Cromwell came the word went out to all the Irish Catholics; "To Hell or to Conaught". This meant that the only place they would be able to find any relief was in the far western province of the island where the land was poor. He destroyed all monasteries he could find. He offered the people of Drogheda and Wexford terms of surrender only to let his troops in to pillage and slaughter as many as they could get their blood stained hands on. He said afterwards, "I am persuaded that this is a righteous judgment of God upon these barbarous wretches, who have imbrued their hands in so much innocent blood and that it will tend to prevent the effusion of blood for the future, which are satisfactory grounds for such actions, which otherwise cannot but work remorse and regret".

His troops went about the countryside committing some of the most dastardly atrocities on men women and children that could only be compared with that of savage Mongols. I will spare the reader the details but suffice it to say that when it came to the slaughter of children the common saying was "nits breed lice".

After he had finished his war to kill as many Catholics as he could, the famine brought on purposely by the burning of crops and then the pestilence that followed made Ireland truly a land of sorrows. "The curse of Crummel be on ya", was what would be called down on someone you hated even up to modern times. Thousands left either voluntarily or were "transported" to the four corners of the world. In the next century Australia was set up as a penal colony and the Irish became the dominant population.

THE RISING

Tis the most distressful country that ever could be seen,
Sure their hangin men and women for the wearin of
the Green.

The rising of the Moon

I n the late 1700's two tremendous events took place on both
sides of the ocean that would eventually change the course of
all of human history. Thirteen upstart English colonies in the
Americas demanded representation in Parliament if the mother
country was going to pass laws regarding them. The dispute over
taxes grew into what eventually became open conflict and the
"Thirteen Colonies" with significant help from France won their
independence and became a free nation.

This was exactly what Ireland wanted. They wanted the right of
self determination; to be able to govern oneself and not be ruled
by another nation. But unfortunately that other nation was only
a short distance across the Irish Sea from them and not 3,000
miles away across the Atlantic Ocean.

Then in 1789 the peasants of France rose up against the aristocracy but this was unlike the American Revolution, which was
really the "American War for Independence". This was more of

an internal revolt with most of the army siding with the revolutionaries. They began executing the nobility and clergy as well as anyone related to or involved with them in the least way. The king and queen weren't spared the guillotine. Chaos resulted with one group taking over and executing their rivals only to be denounced as traitors to the revolution by some other faction and then be on their way to the "steel mistress". It was "The Reign of Terror".

Inspired by the success of America and France, a group called the United Irishmen rose up in rebellion. This time the organization was comprised of Protestants and Catholics who felt as though they were Irishmen together and wanted a republic free of all potentates and nobles.

One of their leaders, a Protestant named Theabold Wolf Tone had arranged for French ships to land troops and weapons at Bantry Bay in Kerry in December of 1796. Wolf Tone arrived off the coast with a French fleet and 14,000 veteran French troops. As fortune would have it constant storms as well as bad leadership kept them from landing and they returned to France.

The "Rising of '98" took place and spread throughout the island although mixed communications and informers took away the ability to coordinate and any element of surprise. Throughout the history of Ireland, more victories were won by English gold than by English steel since informers were easily bought given the poverty of the country.

The British realized that the best thing they could do was to sow animosity between the Protestants and the Catholics especially in Ulster where a large number of Catholics and Protestant Presbyterians, had found common cause. They succeeded in dividing the Irish by religion which is still evident to this day. They then issued Martial Law and went about burning houses and torturing prisoners. Murder and the use of the "pichcap" and "half hanging" were common.

The English showed that nothing seemed below them when it came to winning in war. They used scorched earth policies with the intent of bringing on famine and pestilence which was the usual result. They used biological warfare against American Indian tribes by intentionally spreading small pox among them during the French and Indian Wars and also against the Colonial troops during The American Revolution.

They considered the Irish to be "savages" as they had labeled the Native Americans. Dehumanizing them made it easier to excuse the use of cruel treatment and even elimination. Such philosophy and programs would raise their ugly heads again in another time and another place.

In August of 1798 three French ships sailed into Killala Bay at Kilcummin and dropped anchor off the village of Clougher, where I was born. There were 1,000 seasoned French soldiers led by Gen. Humbert. They brought muskets and pikes to arm the people.

Over 5,000 volunteers flocked to their side and after camping for the night near Kilcummin Head the small army of smartly uniformed well disciplined French troops and a host of "rag-tag" Irish peasants set off down the road to Killala where there was a garrison of British troops. I like to think that one of my ancestors took up either musket or pike and marched off down the road to the sound of a French drum. Maybe one of the leaves of my family tree fell in one of the battles that took place during that short but glorious attempt at freedom.

They routed the small contingent of British troops at Killala then Ballina and the enemy ran so fast at the battle of Castlebar that it came to be known as "The Races at Castlebar". There they set up a make shift "Republic of Ireland". But eventually time had run out and a large army under the command of none other than Lord Cornwallis, unscathed by his humiliating defeat at Yorktown Virginia, caught up with them.

In the ensuing Battle of Ballinamuck, Humbert's army was far outnumbered. The French surrendered and were given all the military courtesies accorded by the rules of war, as they looked on helplessly as their Irish allies, to whom surrender meant the hangman's rope or exile, stood their ground and were hacked to pieces on the field. Ironically much of this was carried out by Scottish Highlanders who spoke Gaelic not English just like the Irishmen that they were slaughtering. The leaders of The Rising which included priests were captured and hanged.

The risings in other areas were quickly put down although some guerilla warfare continued for several more years in the Wiklow Mountains. As usual the repercussions were brutal. Fr. John Murphy, who trained for the priesthood in Spain, at first spoke up against the rebellion. He changed his mind when his parishioners came to him for protection against the yoemenry that were terrorizing the area. He and other leaders successfully led men armed mostly with pikes against British soldiers. He and James Gallager were eventually captured and tortured for information. Then Fr. Murphy was stripped, flogged, hung, and beheaded. His body was burned in a barrel of tar and his head displayed on a pike for all to see the results of rebellion against the crown.

The British felt they could put an end to all this by taking away any autonomy left to what was called the British Ascendancy. They were the descendents of the English who had settled and kept apart from the Irish and belonged to the approved Church of Ireland. England felt that their treatment of the Irish as well as the United Irishmen was the cause for the rebellion. In 1800 Parliament passed The Act of Union making Ireland part of Great Britain. Now it would be known as the "Kingdom of Great Britain and Ireland".

A move for Catholic Emancipation began to take effect in Britain and Ireland. Slowly the laws persecuting Catholics began to be relaxed but economic inequality was still a problem. Daniel O'Connell was elected to Parliament despite his not being allowed to sit legally. This impressed one of the best champions for Catholic Emancipation, none other than Arthur Wellesley the Duke of Wellington and hero of the battle of Waterloo.

He was one of the British Ascendancy born in Ireland to English aristocracy. He was a brilliant military tactician and an inveterate snob. He rarely spoke to his servants, preferring to leave them notes. When once reminded by a journalist that he was born in Ireland, he replied, "Because one is born in a stable does not make one a horse".

When he became Prime Minister of England his term was marked for his efforts to give the Catholics in Ireland and England relief from the terrible restrictions and prejudice placed upon them. He took much criticism for trying to bring this about. He was even accused by The Earl of Winchilsea of "an insidious design for the infringement of our liberties and the introduction of Popery into every department of the State". For this Wellington challenged him to a duel which ended out like most of the duels with nobody being shot and the Earl apologizing for his remarks.

But Wellington pushed through the Catholic Relief Act of 1829 and publicly announced that he would resign if King George IV didn't sign it. Just as at Waterloo, he won. The Penal Laws were dismantled and the Roman Catholic Relief Act of 1829 removed most of the restrictions on Catholics in Britain and Ireland. Requirements to renounce any authority of the Pope and belief in Transubstantiation were removed.

THE GREAT FAMINE
- AN GORTA MÓR

Weary men what reap ye? -
Golden corn for the stranger.
What sow ye? -
Human corpses that wait for the avenger.
Fainting forms, hunger stricken,
what see you in the offing?
Stately ships to bear our food away,
amid the stranger's scoffing.

The Famine Year by Jane Francesca Wilde

I reland was by no means free from its oppressors. Economically Ireland existed for one purpose and for one purpose only; the benefit of the mother country. The system is known as Mercantilism. Everything from India to Canada; from Australia and Africa, from Caribbean islands to Singapore, Hong Kong and their protectorates in China all existed for England. "The Sun never set on the British Empire". During the 18th and 19th century they presented an aura of civility and refinement to the world that was belied by their actions. It was the "Georgian" and "Victorian Era" and all the proprieties of civilized society were the norm. They believed in Kipling's poem, "The White Man's Burden". They felt that they, as "White" people had an obligation to bring the coloured people of the world to civilization.

While suppressing the slave trade, with many well intentioned religious and social leaders in England to foster it, they also helped eliminate any competition to the workers in the mines and factories of the fledgling Industrial Revolution back home. These workers; men women and children were little more than slaves themselves sometimes seeing the light of day only on Sunday.

They had no problem with people of color whom they called "Wogs" as servants and laborers whether in the tea fields of India or the diamond mines of South Africa. While patrolling the seas to eliminate the slave trade, they also were supporting the Confederate cause in the American Civil War. Slaves were used for the cotton trade and cotton was essential to the British textile industry. Southern blockade runners would bring cotton to England and return with arms and supplies.

They pursued a program to make China accept their presence in lucrative trading cities. The Opium Wars forced the Chinese to import opium shipped by the powerful British East India Company from India to China eventually enslaving millions to the pipe. Chinese Junks of wood were little opposition to ironclad ships of the line. The British simply blew them out of the water.

After The First Opium War, (1839-1842), the British received Hong Kong in perpetuity along with five of what was known as "Treaty Cities". The next year they received most favored nation status. France followed suit securing the same concessions in 1843 and 1844. The Second Opium War secured the opium trade and "Coolie" trade and more concessions opening all of China to British merchants. Of course France demanded the same as the British. Eventually eighty treaty ports were set up throughout China by different foreign powers including Germany, Japan and the United States.

The face that the English showed to the world gave the impression of the epitome of civilization and culture. Next door to them the Irish were impoverished and in dire need. They were reduced to living on bare essentials and the most important crop that they depended on was the potato. For many it was their one and only meal for the day.

Famine was not new to Ireland. With crop burning that came along with the many wars starvation wasn't unknown to them. Then in the eighteenth century climate changes brought about famine as well. In 1709, there came a blast of cold weather that ruined crops in northern Europe and was devastating to the Irish. In 1740 to 1741 during what was called "The Great Frost", more Irish people perished than during the great potato famine in the 1840's. This was mainly due to the fact that few people at that time could afford to immigrate. But the English closed the ports to exports of needed food and did what they could to control the price of grain in order to help the starving people.

For the British, Ireland was a bread basket; the land of milk and honey and beef. By the nineteenth century most of the good land had been given over to grazing for the consumer market in England. Cows were more important than people. The English market for Irish beef was insatiable. The grain and dairy products as well as pork, mutton and wool were vital to the English economy especially considering the short distance of transport.

This had a devastating effect on the Irish people. They were forced off the best land and on to small plots of unfavorable land. They depended on the potato; a crop easily grown in poor soil and below the ground sheltered from harsh weather. It was their main means of survival.

Then in 1845 there came a blight that swept through Europe destroying the potato crops. The potatoes turned to black melted mush in the fields. For the rest of Europe it wasn't as bad since most depended on grains and other vegetables as well as what meat they could afford.

To the Irish it was a disaster. This was all they had to eat, and there was very little relief from their "Mother Country". The ports remained open and the export of vital food stuffs kept leaving the starving country to fatten the gentry of Great Britain. The amount of money spent for relief was 7 million pounds. The English had paid 30 million pounds to the planters of the West Indies in compensation for freeing their slaves.

The British didn't want to upset the balance of trade. In Parliament the dominant party was all for Mercantilism and Laissez-faire. Great quantities of food were exported even during the worst years of the famine. Some exports actually increased during this time. Evictions also increased causing great suffering.

Many of the English landlords rarely visited their holdings and some had never set foot in Ireland so the plight of the people was of little consequence to them. They were concerned about collecting rents and being taxed by the government. Military guards were used as food was shipped from the most stricken areas in the West. Food riots broke out in various places with sometimes deadly results.

Word got out around the world of what was happening in Ireland. Contributions came from many countries but it wasn't enough to end the starvation. Queen Victoria sent £2,000. The Sultan of the Ottoman Empire offered £10,000 but was asked by either British diplomats or his own advisers to lower it to £1,000 so he wouldn't embarrass the Queen. Pope Pius IX and the Czar of Russia sent money. President Polk and Abraham Lincoln who was then a Congressman sent donations. The Irish soldiers in the British army together with the Irish workers for the East India Company sent £14,000. Religious and secular organizations like The British Relief Association raised money in England, Australia and America and with the help of the "Queen's Letter" they raised some £390,000 for assistance to Ireland.

Even the Choctaw Nation in Oklahoma after suffering their own plight by being driven from their land and enduring "The Trail of Tears" just 16 years earlier sent 170 dollars. This gesture is remembered by both nations and is a bond between them to this day. Other organizations like the Quakers tried to fill the gap and the government reinstated relief work. But the food supplies were slow in coming.

The people were reduced to eating nettles, berries, seaweed, roots, shellfish, weeds and sometimes even grass. Children cried endlessly from malnutrition. Gaunt skeletal figures in rags with sunken eyes roamed the roads aimlessly in search of anything to eat dropping dead in their tracks. Travelers and journalists from England reported horrible sights. Dead bodies lay along the roads unburied and being eaten by dogs and pigs. Their sketches of children in rags scraping for roots in a field as well as the picture of a mother with her dead baby in her arms begging for money to buy a small coffin touched people around the world.

The winter of 1846-47 was the worst in memory. Blizzards brought snow reaching up to the roofs of the cottages. Because of the relatively mild climate due to the Gulf Stream, Ireland usually gets snow only in higher elevations in the winter time. This year was different with a change in the prevailing winds bringing snow, sleet and hail.

This was more than anyone could take and immigration soared. When the blight had passed and the potato crop came back over a million people had starved to death and two million had left the country. The island was devastated.

There is great controversy both historically and politically of whether or not the English policy during the famine amounted to genocide. Surely the increase in evictions could constitute a good argument for the case alone.

In 1996 a law professor at the University of Illinois, Francis A. Boyle wrote a report commissioned by the New York-based Irish Famine/Genocide Committee. In it he wrote, *"Clearly, during the years 1845 to 1850, the British government pursued a policy of mass starvation in Ireland with intent to destroy in substantial part the national, ethnic and racial group commonly known as the Irish People... Therefore during the years 1845 to 1850 the British Government carried on a policy of mass starvation in Ireland that constituted acts of Genocide against the Irish people within the meaning of Article II © of the 1948 [Hague] Genocide Convention"*. Also in 1996 New Jersey included the Irish famine in the "Holocaust and Genocide Curriculum" at the secondary tier.

Journalist Peter Duffy wrote that, *"The government's crime, which deserves to blacken its name forever"*, was rooted *"in the effort to regenerate Ireland"* through *"landlord-engineered replacement of tillage plots with grazing lands"* that *"took precedence over the obligation to provide food... for its starving citizens. It is little wonder that the policy looked to many people like genocide."*

The famine passed and the people that had survived were left stunned. No one had escaped the horror. Men women and children were left with memories sights and sounds that human beings are not meant to experience. The memories of loved ones especially children crying themselves to death from starvation in their parents arms as well as the wailing at the many gravesites with lines waiting to bury their dead after a few prayers from an exhausted priest is enough to break even the hardest heart.

Why had this happened? Was this the way a "Mother Country" treated her "Children"? Would the reaction from Parliament have been the same if this tragedy had struck Scotland or Wales? Suppose something like this or some other plague came upon Ireland in the future? If the government's reaction was the same it would surely be the end of the Irish people. What had they done to deserve this? Was it because they refused to be ruled by a foreign power or to give up the Holy Faith of their fathers?

Any Irishman would be hard pressed to show any good that came out of being part of the United Kingdom of Great Britain and Ireland. What mother leaves her children to starve to death? The results of the famine only reinvigorated the call for freedom from this cruel oppressive nation that had taken virtually everything of value from them. They replaced their laws, their culture, and their language. The one thing that they could not replace and which was the thread that held the fabric of Ireland together was their Faith.

Many of the upper classes started movements toward "Home Rule". This would have given Ireland the same status as Canada, Australia and other Commonwealth countries. Parliament began considering such an arrangement on and off depending on which party was in power. As far as the Northern Protestants of Ulster were concerned there was no way they would accept such a deal with the majority of the population of the entire island Catholic. They chanted, "Home Rule is Rome Rule". Their blind hatred for anything Catholic still divides the nation with an attitude that is more reminiscent of the 16th century.

For the lower classes, the subsistence farmer as well as the landless outcasts, they wanted nothing to do with England. They were through with Kings and Queens and nobility. They wanted a democratic republic in which they could govern themselves. The whole concept of royalty and nobility has gone its course and is a primitive thing of the past. The very idea of one group of people considering themselves superior to everyone else is archaic to say the least.

A person would think that in this day and age such thinking would be condemned. Instead, "Royalty" is lauded and loved which makes the "Commoner" status acceptable to the masses thus admitting that these so called Nobles are better in some way than the rest of us just by mere chance of birth. Isn't this elitist?

Isn't this opposed to any universal concept of equality?

This, to me seems ridiculous in that these people do not accomplish anything worth while. They don't sing or dance, nor do they create any form of art. They are not scientists or philosophers or inventors. Some of them don't even have any real power except that of status.

Royalty is like keeping very expensive pets only instead of fancy kennels or stables they have palaces and castles. How many palaces and castles do they need? They cost the people millions and produce nothing in return except perhaps revenue from tourists gawking at them. They claim to do a lot of "charity work", but to abdicate their vaunted and exclusive lifestyle would do more for charity than all their fund raising. They consider themselves to be "Blue Bloods". Spiders have blue blood, so the title is fitting.

How did they achieve such honors and wealth? Somewhere in their family history there was a thug that was better at organizing other thugs to steal whatever they desired that belonged to someone else and kill them if they tried to stop them. War is based on theft. All of nobility's wealth is based on plunder be it land or goods. They achieved such great wealth and power because their ancestors stole it. They never earned a dime of it. At this point in time Royalty simply invests part of their stolen treasure or money from taxes in the stock market and off shore banks.

Note that I am not singling out the British Royalty and so called nobility alone. I denounce all Monarchies whether they wield power or not; whether Asian, African or European. The very titles accorded them like, Your Highness, Your Majesty, My Lord or My Lady and the dogmatic belief in "The Divine Right of Kings" is virtually blasphemous. These are titles that belong to God alone and Mary the mother of Christ. I find it hard to find a word to describe what this concept of royalty and nobility is to me. It seems so primitive, prejudiced and unethical. The only word I can think of is that it is Un-American; - *"We hold these truths to be self-evident, that all men are created equal'.*

The rest of the 19th century brought more uprisings with the usual results. The beginning of the 20th century brought more negotiations for Home Rule. Six of the counties in Ulster with Protestant majorities wanted to stay part of the British Empire. Then in 1914 World War I began and everything was put on hold until after the war.

THE WAR FOR INDEPENDENCE

Oh the bravest fell, and the Requiem bell
rang mournfully and clear.
For those who died that Eastertide
in the springtime of the year.
While the world did gaze, with deep amaze,
at those fearless men, but few
Who bore the fight that freedom's light
Might shine in the Foggy Dew.

Fr. Charles O,Neil

T aking advantage of the "Great War", in 1916 the Irish rose
up once more against the English. After the Easter Rebellion and it's suppression by the British, a large amount of
Dublin was destroyed. The IRA, (Irish Republican Army), carried
on a guerrilla war against the Brits. When World War I ended in
1919, England found itself with a glut of unemployed veterans
and a big problem in Ireland. At Churchill's suggestion, who at the
time was British Secretary of State for War, they raised volunteers to fight the war in Ireland.

These men were desperate for employment and after having lived through the horrors of trench warfare they were hard no-nonsense combat veterans who still had the stench of death in their nostrils. Because of a shortage in uniforms they were given black tunics of the Royal Irish Constabulary and kaki trousers from regular army issue. They became the hated "Black and Tans".

With little discipline they freely used reprisals against civilian populations in retaliation for any of their losses to the IRA. They sacked and burned many towns and villages as well as being strongly suspected in the murder of a priest, Father Michael Griffin, in Galway. In December of 1920 they sacked Cork and destroyed a large part of the city center keeping firemen and other emergency units from doing their jobs, sometimes with gunfire.

The war touched Kilcummin as well. The IRA burned the Coast Watchers station at the pier in the village of Clougher. My father, who was just a boy at the time, saw Black and Tans roaming the countryside on patrols, shooting cattle in the fields for "target practice".

His cousin was in the IRA. At the back of the house was a "reek" of hay which is an elongated hay stack. Most of the farm houses in Ireland have these to feed their stock. The one at the back of my grandfather's house was hollowed out in the middle and supported by planks of wood. My father's cousin would stay there overnight or for a few days while "on the run". My grandfather and his eldest son John, would take him out fishing during the day usually lying in the bottom of the boat. Sometimes there would be signs that two or more of them had spent the night there. It was a "safe house".

Finally the British had enough and their policies in Ireland were never totally supported by the British people. The IRA had fought them to a standstill. They called for peace talks and a solution to this seemingly endless problem. On the Irish side some were willing to settle for Home Rule as a step toward independence, while others would settle for nothing less than a complete break with England.

Michael Collins, one of the leaders of the IRA was chosen to head the delegation to London. With threats and promises he accepted the status of Home Rule and signed a treaty of peace which recognized what would be called the Irish Free State. Ireland would have the status of Commonwealth like Canada and Australia with the English monarch on the currency and still swearing allegience to the Crown. Many were tired of the endless fighting and wanted only peace but to others the terms were totally unacceptable.

Collins returned to Ireland with British style uniforms as well as weapons and armored cars. The inevitable happened. Just as in so many cases of a nations fight for independence, there was a struggle for leadership and power. The civil war that broke out was even more bloody and vindictive than the War for Independence. The Free State government had a great advantage over the rebels with artillary, armored cars and machine guns. Civil wars are always an ugly affair with families divided in loyalty. Fellow Irishmen were imprisoning and executing fellow Irishmen on a scale that even the Brits had not engaged in during "The Troubles". Collins himself was killed by his former IRA brothers in arms in an ambush.

After two years of fighting the Free State was victorious. Many still couldn't accept the situation as it was and worked toward a political solution to gain total independance. Eventually the party known as Sinn Fein which was the political arm of the IRA won a majority of seats in the Irish parliament in Dublin over Fine Geal the Free State supporters.

They eliminated the oath of allegiance to the crown and Eamon DeVellara, the Prime Minister, declared the Irish Free State ended and the new independent nation of Eire the Republic of Ireland was proclaimed in 1937. King George VI sent a letter that would almost be called congratulatory to DeVellara stating the long relationship between the two nations.

Sinn Fein had won total independence for the first time in Irish history, and they did it by using ballots and not bullets. Granted this couldn't have been achieved without the hundreds of years of bloody violence, but the peaceful turnover was notable at a time when the rest of Europe was in political turmoil.

For the first time in Ireland's long history the people were living in peace. Six counties in Ulster chose to remain part of Great Britain which is still a bone of contention to this day. Now a person could walk the length and breath of Eire, without being accosted, stepping aside or having to doff their cap to anyone. Now the future of "Inis Fáil - The Island of Destiny" would be determined by a free an independent people.

The End

Printed in Great Britain
by Amazon